DIAMOND GIRL

BY
DEANNA BRUBAKER

Copyright © 2023 Deanna Brubaker

All rights reserved. No part of this publication may be reproduced, distributed, or transmitted in any form or by any means, including photocopying, recording, or other electronic or mechanical methods, without the prior written permission of the publisher, except in the case of brief quotations embodied in critical reviews and certain other noncommercial uses permitted by copyright law.

Contents

Prologue 4
The Beginning 9
Religion 12
Hope 14
Life is Beautiful 17
Marriage and Abuse 20
Sunshine 32
Backslide 37
Dirty Dancing 42
Parental Instincts 47
Single Mom Status 56
Exploited 61
Hmmm…I Can't Remember 66
Drugged Or What? 67
Betrayal 72
The Darkest Hour 76
Fake Beginnings 85
Gateway Drug 87
Trapped 90
A New Job 92
Kidnapped 97
Masters Commission 100
God, Is That You? 106
A lifeline 113

You've Got a Friend	115
The Devils Snare	127
Intervention #2	130
One Good Choice Can Save Your Life	132

Prologue

Family is precious. Husband Jared, kids, Christian Victoria Benjamin, son-in-law Donny and our crown jewel baby Donny. Parents Joseph and Rhonda Merrill, brothers Landon, Stephen, and Nathaniel. My sister in laws Emily, Brunna, and Tia. My nieces and nephews are Owen, Ethan, Bella, Jethro, Emery, Adele, and Sophia. My fantastic in laws Rocky and Vicky and the strong, loyal, fun-loving Brubaker clan, I love you all to the moon and back.

I have learned over the years of being a Pastor at Covenant Church Lake Havasu that I grow, the team grows, and the individuals on the team grow; when I, as the leader, stay in prayer every week. I pray about what to do next and how God wants to lead us.

If I stay in a position of humility and hunger for His way and not mine, we all continue to grow. So, I want to keep growing and moving forward in every department of my life. Also, having the next generation on the team is paramount to leading and leaving a legacy.

I plan to get my Benjamin, our nine-year-old, up there singing alongside me and everyone else. He loves to sing and isn't as shy as my other two.

My passion is worship. It always has been and always will be. One day I hope to be able to pass the torch on to my kids;

wouldn't that be amazing? God knows the desires of your heart and wants them for you just as much as you want them.

Even though I was born basically with a mic in my hand at Gateway Bible college, my parents said they used to have to bribe me with candy to get me up to sing at church.

There is a VHS tape out there of me at three years old with a handmade red velvet dress on with white lace trim, a black welch hat, and matching black patent leather shoes and frilly white socks. My first song to sing in just was

1 John 4:7-8. 7 Beloved, let us [a]love one another: for [b]love is of God; and every one that loveth is [c]born of God, and knoweth God. 8 He that loveth not [a]knoweth not God; for God is love.

I tapped my foot and held the mic perfectly while my mom played the upright piano in my grandfather's start-up church in Wales, England.

The bribery worked because now I am hooked on leading people into worship. I am in the presence of God Most High, where I am at home. A sanctuary of praise, a tabernacle of worship where I have found a home.

It never gets easy. I take worship as a gift and an opportunity. I am a perfectionist and have yet to achieve my goal of a perfect solo or service. I still get weak in the knees, nauseous, and have shortness of breath right before the music starts.

My life is filled with singing, church singing, and secular singing. I've competed and won all different genres and competitions from Maine to Arizona. However, becoming a worshipper…not just singing but creating an atmosphere of worship, is my jam.

I fell in love with who God is. The personal relationship with The Creator is the realist relationship I have ever had or will ever have.

His Holy Spirit is a must, and without it, I am a wanderer.

I'll bounce back and forth in time in this story. It could be titled "The Prodigal Daughter" or "A series of unfortunate events," but having been on the other side of the cross, I can now see the rainbow of hope through every trial and storm.

This is a book about family. A story of redemption and forgiveness. A lesson on addiction.

Prayer

Lord, help whoever is reading this to hear your voice. Only you know what is deep in every heart. Let this story be an example of how good You are.

Amen

German philosopher **Friedrich Nietzsche's**
"What does not kill me makes me stronger."

Diamond girl used to be an outreach my mother started in our community. It was a nonprofit for single moms. It is true diamonds are a girl's best friend. Who would say no to a diamond? Hidden under the earth's mantle miles from the surface, a diamond is created after many years under immense pressure and extreme heat.

Life is hard. The pressure and hard times you have been through have made you the toughest gem on the planet. Diamonds are virtually indestructible. As hard as things get it, as tough as life is, you can get through it and possibly reflect even more light than anyone else. Diamonds reflect the light.

The Beginning

John 1 1, In the beginning, was the Word, and the Word was with God, and the Word was God.

² The same was in the beginning with God.

³ All things were made by him; and without him was not anything made that was made.

⁴ In him was life; and the life was the light of men.

⁵ And the light shineth in darkness; and the darkness comprehended it not

I love God. He was good for me. I knew He created me. I was born during my parents' education in a seminary in St. Louis, Mo. September 1980. Born into ministry, raised in the Word, being a Christian was all godfathered into my life. I am third a generation Pastor. My sprawling family is brimming with pastors, teachers, missionaries, evangelists, songwriters and performing artists, church planters, and authors.

When I was young, we lived in small-town Maine. My parents were young and indoctrinated in the United Pentecostal religion, along with everyone I knew.

My father has 5 siblings, and my mother has 4 with some foster home siblings as well; one imp particular we still keep in contact with.

Life was simple in Maine, and I loved playing with my cousins at my grandparents' house. Grammy's house was located in the same parking lot as the church. It was built by my grandfather.

This church is still a church in our family and is thriving today as I write this. The house beside the church is called the parsonage, where I have some fun memories of making puppet shows at Christmas time.

We played hide and seek in the church while all the adults visited the parsonage and cooked. We would hide under pews, behind the baptism tank, and in Sunday school rooms; it was a blast. Sometimes, we would turn all the lights off to make it even more fun.

We soon got hungry and bundled back up to go over to the house where the family was. Nighttime came, and while the adults were upstairs, Becky and Jonathan, my brothers, and myself played in the basement. It is memories like this in our childhood that we can hold on to and cherish. Good memories have a nostalgic side effect.

Religion

There were some weird rules in the Uninted Pentecostal Organized religion; most of the rules were for us girls. We couldn't wear pants, even in the cold, with no makeup, and our hair couldn't be cut. I was young and didn't know that making these life choices was a big deal because everyone I knew lived the same way.

As I got older, I noticed I was different from other girls at school. I didn't understand why the strict regulation, why didn't we have a tv, why didn't we listen to radio music like my friends' parents. The only explanation I remember them saying is that it made us better Christians. It taught us to rely on God and not the world. To this day, after all my theology classes and self-study of the Word, all the sermons, and most importantly, my close relationship with God, the U.P.C. way doesn't make sense to me.

My parents wouldn't stay much longer after this Christmas being U.P.C. Now, today we are followers of Jesus Christ, plain and simple. We live our life by the Bible. If you want a title for our beliefs, it would be non-denominational with the good roots of pentecostal.

I have learned that every tribe is different. I won't judge my family for their strictness or label others weird because of their personal convictions about life without conveniences, but it's definitely not the route I am taking to heaven.

At the time, I had two little brothers. Landon a sandy blonde, thick-haired, big blue-eyed preacher slash comedian, and Stephen is a lighted blonde-haired blue/green-eyed, big cheeked tender-hearted boy. Then, three days after my 11th birthday, my third baby brother was born. Nathaniel. He had big blue eyes with black hair and long eyelashes, he didn't look like us three kids at all, and we loved him so much. The family was and is still everything to me.

DIVE DEEP

Food for thought: Every person has a longing to belong within them. What kind of people are you drawn to? Are they happy? Are they energetic? Are they family born or selected?

_____
_____
_____
_____
_____
_____
_____

Hope

No matter what your religion or beliefs are, hope is what keeps a human alive in this world. Without hope, we have seen and heard of the devastating things that a person can do to themselves or those around them.

Hope is a heart thing. When you have heartbreak, hope can seem far away. Not one person can make it through a whole lifetime without a heartbreak of some kind. It could be a physical diagnosis, a financial pitfall, a broken marriage, rejection from someone, adultery, death of a loved one, or death of a dream or future. A broken heart could occur from a title we never wanted or thought we would have. It's a relentless pain and an unceasing sorrow. It haunts and taunts without consideration of the love lost.

The depth of an emotional wound with no seemingly end in sight is a heart without hope. A heart without hope cannot resist the emotional paralysis that slips in uninvited. It renders up unable to move and brings darkness upon the soul. It takes a breath from the body, life from the spirit, and hope from the heart.

Three tell-tale signs you may have a heartbreak.
1. Lack of self-worth
2. Lack of intimacy with others
3. Lack of intimacy with God

The common theme here is the word LACK. Every place in the Bible that talks about lack of or not enough of or going without a miracle happens, and the people are given more than enough.

Empty pots filled with oil. The water turned into wine. Boats filled with fish. Five loaves and 2 fish feeding a multitude with take home left over. God is not a God of lack! PERIOD! There is healing and hope for you. There is reason to GO ON!
HEALING within REACH.

Jesus is close to the brokenhearted he has compassion for those who are hurt. God gives and never stops giving and providing for His children; you are no exception.

In the midst of a broken heart, GOD has a purpose and wisdom to pull you through. Jesus binds up our wounds. Blessed are brokenhearted, for they will be comforted.

Prayer

I am a follower of you, Jesus Christ. I have HOPE that You are holding on to me even when I am a drift. All of my lack will no longer be lacking in any area because you see the need and hear my cry. I give you all of my cares and deepest hurts. I receive your healing goodness, and thank you for providing and filling my cup running over.

Amen

Life is Beautiful

Present time I am standing at the sink doing dishes and looking out of the little window above the sink into my front yard. I see the hummingbirds sucking the nectar from our honey suckle tree, and I take a deep breath in and exhale joyfully.

A quail family comes running across the driveway to get shelter under the tree and eat the fallen pedals. A little gray bunny hops across the pavers and up onto the fountain in the middle of our front yard. I think to myself; I love this house! I love animals!

I love Arizona! I love my husband! I love my church! What a great life I have! I have been given so much! My mind goes down the list of thankful.

My husband, my hero, flipped this amazing house for us to enjoy. It has the pool & spa we always wanted. It is modern and cozy all at the same time. I love the fireplace he designed himself, and his older brother Grant who passed away from Leukemia, built this fireplace, so it is extra special.

We have three kids; my little bears are healthy and doing big things. Christian, my oldest, is in the Navy. He has a ministerial calling in his life, and he knows it. I am excited to see what God does. I always tell people he was my first heartbeat because when he was born, I felt the deepest love I had never known until I held him. I am a proud Navy mom.

Our only daughter Victoria is getting her pilot's license and is married to an awesome, kind young man named Donald.

Together Donny and Tori, my son-in-law and daughter, have given me one of life's most precious gifts. A grandson, his name is Donald Von Tatham III. Big name for a baby, but he is going to grow into it and do big things. Tori is smarter and prettier than I ever was. She has this drive and focuses in her that I am continuously inspired by.

Benjamin is the youngest and is a soccer fanatic. He brings boundless energy everywhere he goes. He is as smart as a tack and good at anything he tries. He has a marked amount of passion and talent.

Life is great. God is good!

It wasn't always good. Let me tell you about what has happened to me and my choices along the way.

I have tried really hard to be a good person and fell flat on my face many times. I used to blame God and others for my misfortune, but I have now realized that I was the problem.

My responses and attitude towards things that happened in my life caused me to make poor choices. You will, at some point, be reminded of a hard time you have gone through yourself.
I don't know why I got a second and third chance. I certainly don't deserve it. I do know this.

I trust God is able to fix, restore and redeem any and all! I know from experience that He is real. Even in the darkest times in my story, He never left me for some reason.

DIVE DEEP

WHERE IN YOUR PAST CAN YOU SEE A TIME WHEN GOD KEPT YOU SAFE OR PROTECTED?

_____
_____
_____
_____
_____
_____
_____
_____

Marriage and Abuse

The policeman was taking my info. I was stunned, dazed. I sat in my little living room in Dallas, Texas. It was an adorable first home. Craftsman-style home with a cute front yard and big backyard with a wood fence. The garage was in the back of the house, so it had an adorable curb appeal. Red brick and light blue paneling on the outside and on the inside. The previous owner happened to be a carpenter and used this house to show his talent. It was beautiful with so much character. I loved this house. It was perfect for us.

My mother was sitting on the coffee table, and my two babies were in the back room. The officer stood in my living room, taking down the information about the fight that happened between my husband and me. I was 22 my thoughts were everywhere and nowhere all at once while he was talking.

I remember the officer taking pictures of my face and neck. I remember how the room felt, empty and cold. The officer began to inform me that I could file a protective order and change the locks, or I could let him leave with the report and file it away for record keeping. I was quiet. Usually, when forced to make a snap decision, I panic, but my heart is barely beating. I don't even remember breathing. Am I breathing?

As I sat there, I had a vision I'll never forget. I looked out the back window past my mom, past the officer beyond the living room, and through the dining room to the sliding glass door to the grassy backyard. I got a glimpse of my future without seeing what was physically there. It was as if someone had me peering down the lens of looking glass into my life into my future.

I saw her, me, sitting in the same house, same situation, same position on the couch. An officer was standing over me, asking me more questions, the same type of questions. What happened, what do you want to do about it, etc. In this vision, I was older. I would guess forty-ish. I had bags under my eyes. My hair was thinning, I had not aged well, and I looked so much older. I felt sad for the woman I saw.

I came back to real-time reality and looked up at the officer who had been waiting to hear a response. I thought if I changed the locks to the house like he suggested and put a restraining order on my husband, he was going to get mad, and it would be the beginning of the end.

I didn't want a divorce. No one in my family was divorced. We had one rebel uncle out of all of them who had gotten divorced a few times, but everyone else was deep into faith and would not be ok with me getting divorced. I had self-inflicted pressure to stay married for the family's honor.

I saved myself for one man I waited for, and now it's all falling apart. I don't want it to end. I realized if I didn't do something now, I was going to be that woman in the future. She was in no shape or form, strong enough to start over. Her future was bleak.

I am young; I have much more energy and life in me. I am strong at 22. I don't want to wait until I'm too weak, too old, and tired to start over. I'd rather do it now. I signed the documents with the officer and changed the locks. My marriage of 2 1/2years was over. I was 22 with two babies. I was oblivious to what was about to happen.

Dallas was massive and full of a variety of people. I was fresh out of high school, class of 1998, with 60ish graduates. "Go, Prairieland Patriots!

We moved from Maine the summer after 6th grade. Houston, Texas, was our first stop where I was home-schooled. Seventh grade moved to the country. Eighth grade was in another town and a new school. I changed schools almost every year since Kindergarten, so being the "new girl" was easy for me. I learned to make friends quick.

By sophomore year God placed us in a magnificent east Texas town called Cunningham. High school years were spent here. Farm country living is peaceful. The parsonage was being built while we lived in the church's fellowship hall. I could flourish and feel at home.

We moved after graduation and said goodbye to my favorite town, the town I feel like I grew up in with my best friend Amber and her family. We set off to the big city.

I went through a little bit of shock and anxiety with all the stores, traffic, and, most of all, trusting people. In Cunningham, everyone knew each other, I mean really knew each other, knew where each other lived, how many animals and acres you had, what church you attended. It was a wonderful, safe haven to raise a family. Dallas was a culture shock.

I enrolled in Community College. While in my humanities class met a tall, older student with tattoos and a tongue ring named Bill. He had a huge smile. He was different from all my church and cowboy friends in the country.

We started seeing each other more and more against my parent's blessing. One night I went out to a club for 18 and older he was there. He was old enough to drink and needed a ride home, so I drove him to his apartment. He was funny and fun and liked me. I started drinking and hanging out with him every day.

I woke up hungover with a blurry memory of the night and what had happened. I wasn't dressed; something had happened. I asked him, and he said yes, that we had been together.

I began to cry; I had been saving myself for marriage. I never was taught about sex. My parents preached abstinence.

Tampons were a no go only pads. The little I did know about I had picked up on by listening to other girls at school. You are supposed to bleed after having your first time. I had not bled. Maybe I am different that others? I was confused, he said we did "it" but my body wasn't showing signs of having lost the one thing I had guarded, saved, protected for my wedding night. I didn't trust him; I barely knew him but he had a way of convincing me. I was young and dumb. I bought about his lie and cried over the issue. I cried because I didn't love him and now, I would have to fall in love with him. I am to marry him. I told myself that the first one is the only one and I am sticking to my plan. I was ashamed. I was disappointed.

Things happen, and we don't know why and maybe we never will. I have learned that God has a moral will. We have the freedom to choose. This freedom is great, but it's also the reason we get hurt.

A bang on the door. I froze! "Deanna!", "Deanna!" a frantic voice was yelling my name. "oh sh*t, it's your mom!" I lept out of bed into the bathroom, straight into the tub, and shut the shower curtain. He ran into the bathroom, quietly shut the door, and whispered to me, "sshh." I heard my mom look in the bedroom (where I am sure she noticed my clothes all over the room & my car parked out front). My life flashed before my eyes. I thought it's over. I am caught bare in a boy's apartment. She is going to kill me.

I heard her on the other side of the bathroom door. She was still yelling my name, then quiet and still. I heard the front door shut. She was gone, and I wasn't busted. Phew!

Beware: When you are young and naïve; you tend to believe everything, you hear. Red flags are hard to see.

I thought I was special enough to make this man stay with me forever turned out he had a girlfriend, and I was the "other woman" I wasn't even done becoming a woman, and yet here I am as "that girl." Even though he soon broke it off with her, the trust was forever broken.

I felt trapped in a future of my own making and my own choosing. Now I had to make sure it became the life I liked. I stayed with him.

My poor parents tried over and over to intervene but to no avail. I was a stubborn young adult. Things got so bad that they had no choice but to kick me out of the house after a physical throwdown altercation.

When my daughter turned18, she wasn't defiant and rebellious like I was. She is so much better than I deserve. She is much smarter and more obedient than me. I can't imagine having a fight with her the way I fought with my parents.

After many red flags and no trust, I called it quits. I started going back to church. I got my first apartment with a girl from church. I started singing alto for the young adult worship team. I had three jobs and went back to school. I was crushing it. I couldn't stay away from him.

I ultimately wanted to make it work. I didn't want to have to explain to anyone that I wasn't a virgin anymore. I was ashamed of that. I couldn't possibly be able to say that to anyone new.

He reached out to me, and we began dating again. He lived with a female friend, I had forbidden him from doing that if he wanted to be with me. He reassured me over and over they were only friends. One day I pulled up to their apartment, his car was parked out front but no one answered. I walked around to the back door. I heard heavy breathing; it was the two of them. I leaned in to be able to hear clearly. I heard moans and groans. I felt my stomach drop to my knees, I banged on the door "Hello?" silence, it wasn't a TV, the real voices I had heard stopped making noise. I slumped down onto the ground, leaned against the door and cried. I am not sure how much time went by before the heavy breathing and sex noises started up again. I felt like I was intruding on my Bill while he cheated on me. He had tricked me again. I was so dumb.

I confronted him later when he finally returned my calls and denied it all. He said I was crazy, jealous and immature. He made me feel bad for not trusting him and threatened to not be with me.

Before I knew it, we were engaged. My parents had no clue and soon after saying yes, I discovered I was pregnant.

It's so obvious to me now all the other things that were missing in this relationship.

DIVE DEEP

When have you ever had to walk away from someone who wasn't good for you? What does a healthy relationship look like to you?

_____
_____
_____
_____
_____
_____
_____

Proverbs   **11:2**

When pride comes, then comes disgrace, but with humility comes wisdom. (NIV)

    I went to my parent's apartment to give them the news. I was still seeing "my first" again. We are engaged. They were going to be grandparents. As I write this, I feel so bad that they had to hear about all of this at the same time.

    As I told them, my mom's eyes lit up with joy. "A baby!" My heart leaped in my chest when she said it. I was so happy, and she was as happy as I was. My dad, however, was crushed. I could see the shock and disappointment on his face. He said, "we can stop this," you can stop the pregnancy, get rid of this guy, and get your life back on track.

I said, "It is too late for that. I love him. I don't believe in abortion, and he proposed to me," why wouldn't I try to set up a family of my own? They could tell my mind was made up. They eventually came to terms with my decision and bless their hearts; they started planning the wedding with me.

The night of Bill's bachelor party, he called me while I was home pregnant. He was telling me everything was going great. He was in the limo; I asked him if his "friends," who were girls, had gone as well? I was hunting to know if one, in particular, was there, the one I had forbidden him to invite. The one I had thought he was still seeing behind my back. We finished the conversation, and I was about to hang up when I heard someone talking in a girl's voice. He thought he hung up but hadn't' so I listened.

I listened for the next 20 minutes to him laugh and talk with friends. They talked about our relationship, and I cried as they made fun of me, the little girl, dumb and pregnant, stupid and naive to believe him, and too young to drink.

I was 19 and felt so pathetic. I agreed I was young and stupid and pregnant. I couldn't believe he was laughing. It hurt me so bad that by the time he got home, I was under so much stress I called my mom to protect him from me and to help me stay calm for my baby.

I screamed, yelled, slapped. My poor mother tried wedging her body between him and me so that I wouldn't go too far. She just kept saying be careful, the baby, the baby.

Our wedding was coming up soon. I needed to calm down and let go so we could have a good wedding.

In the bridal suite, about to walk down the aisle, my mom said, "just because you're pregnant doesn't mean you have to get married." I looked at her and said, "it's too late."

I will marry him, do the right thing for my baby, and bring this child into this world in a happy home with a mom and dad. God is going to keep us together and make this work.

I worshipped in a church service, and tears began to roll down my cheeks as the choir sang. I could feel the presence of God all around me. As I enjoyed the moment, the man I had married leaned in and asked me what was wrong. "What's wrong?! Then I realized, he doesn't know what worship looks like. He doesn't get it or understand God's presence, and he can't feel what I am feeling? This is never going to last. This marriage is doomed.

I am a fool for thinking I could will this relationship into a good one. I hadn't prayed or worshipped like this in so long. I wanted to be able to express my love for God and worship God with a husband who gets me. We are just very different people. This is never going to work.

"The Lord is close to the brokenhearted and saves those who are crushed in spirit."

Christian was born on October 16, 2000. I was induced into labor. I weighed in at 163lbs. All my stretchmarks came from this baby.

When the doctor put him in my arms, the largest amount of love poured over me and filled me. I felt a love that cannot be described. I loved Christian more than I thought humanly possible. It was like I felt my heartbeat for the first time. My big beautiful boy. A blonde hair, brown-eyed baby who loved to snuggle!

Christian made life so beautiful and so worth it. This baby was a gift from God himself. Hope in the form of a child. Everything that had happened all made sense now that I had Christian; he was my life.

Sunshine

September 11, 2000. Bill changed that day. He wanted, to go into the military and defend our country but felt obligated to stay with me and the baby.

Bill started drinking a lot; he began staying out later than usual at the bar. I started getting paranoid. It brought back flashbacks to all the fights we had before marriage. I just wanted him to love me. I wanted what my parents had.

In our bedroom I would later learn in life after knowing real love and respect from a man, that it was a place where I had ben taken advantage of and abused. I was his property not his wife. I was an object for him to do with me what he wanted and when he wanted it. I never knew what real love making was until I married Jared. My purity, my youth and my innocence was stolen by Bill and I let him do it. I let him climb into bed at 2am, 3am or 4am and I tried to be a good wife.

He told me one more baby, maybe this would make everything better. I didn't realize the reason he had asked me for another baby. Bill and his family had convinced each other that I had tricked Bill into marrying me by getting pregnant and that my beautiful baby boy Christian was not in fact his. Bill's family was cruel to me. I was 20 years old and they treated me like a whore. I was a virgin I would explain, its physically impossible for anyone else to be the father. I wanted to tell them that he is the one who tricked me by lying about my "first time" with him. The truth was he told me we did it when we actually had not, it was after I told him I had to marry him that we had intercourse again and that is when I bled for the first time, I ran to the bathroom to clean up initially embarrassed then realizing that I had been doped out of my virginity and how stupid I was to have trusted this guy and now my fate was certainly sealed to marry him. He had tricked me! Not the other way around, but I wouldn't dare say things like this to anyone out of embarrassment.

Another baby? Ok maybe it will fix us. I made him promise me that we would get out of the apartment and buy a home for our growing family.

So, I got pregnant with a baby girl, and he bought us a home. Being pregnant with Tori was so different than with Christian. I was overweight with Christian, and with Tori, I couldn't keep weight on. Morning sickness was all day, every day.

I had a good job as a leasing agent for the apartment complex I used to live in. I kept a trash can and saltine crackers with me at all times. My stress level was so high due to the tumultuous relationship at home, and therefore I was eventually bedridden. I buried the pain of the dysfunctional marriage inside. I thought I could make this work.

Victoria Elizabeth was born on January 29, 2002. She was gorgeous! A perfect little doll.

Late night and early morning fights continued so did my paranoia. More importantly, though, something was wrong with Tori. She wasn't keeping any of her milk down.

I hadn't slept in days, trying to figure out what was wrong. I finally broke down and took her to my mom's house to ask for help. By the time we got Tori to the ER, she had a raging fever. We were going to be sent to St. Jude's Hospital for surgery.

Pyloric Stenosis was her diagnosis. It is when the muscle around the duodenum is enlarged and squeezing the tube shut so that nothing can pass out of the stomach. They performed the surgery to release the muscle.

Staying in the hospital with her was a blessing. I was able to sleep and focus only on her. I thought I would lose her. God saved her life. Tori is stronger than most. She just competed in a cross-fit competition and is such an athlete you would never know looking at her that we had a health scare and almost lost her. The scar on her tummy is barely noticeable. She is truly the most beautiful girl in the world, inside and out. I am so blessed she is alive.

The arguing turned into physical altercations. Slamming me up against the wall. Pulling me out of the shower by my hair. Choking me. I am not going to get into the ugly details of domestic violence. It was bad. It is never ok to put your hands on someone in anger and turn to violence.

I was a fighter; I grew up with 3 brothers. It wasn't all him. I was just as bad. I had changed so much of myself to give this relationship a chance. I changed my hair, my body my relationship with God. I was so far from my true self. I made so many decisions that were just not me. I was mad that no matter what I did, the relationship was destined for destruction. Relationship OVER.

I told the officer sitting there in the living room that it was over I was ready to change the locks and get a protective order. Bill wanted a divorce too he just didn't want to have to pay child support. He wanted the money, I wanted the kids. We agreed.

Life has a way of kicking you when you're down. If you lack self-esteem, you will continue to let it happen. That is when it becomes your fault too. You have to pick yourself up and start over, even if it means going without any of the comforts of life.

"Nothing is impossible; the word itself says 'I'm possible!'"
AUDREY HEPBURN

Backslide

Psalms 14:1-3

1 ^aThe ^bfool hath said in his heart; There is ^cno ^dGod. They are ^ecorrupt, they have done abominable works, there is ^fnone that doeth good. 2 The Lord looked down from heaven upon the children of men, to see if there were any that did understand, and seek God.

Driving down the road, I had a one-sided conversation with God. I said, "God, I know you are for real, but you're not for me anymore. I am so angry that you would let my marriage end in divorce. You didn't protect me!

I did all the right things, and you let me down. You obviously don't care. Right here, I need to stop. Hindsight is 20/20. I know how foolish this sounds. I was blind. I was blinded by fear and doubt. Worst of all, I was brokenhearted and hated this feeling, so instead of crying out to God, I turned my back on Him in anger.

I was blind to how fortunate I was and took my life for granted. I was acting like a spoiled brat.

I changed all the programmed Christian radio stations in my car to alternative music, which was a very big deal for me, considering I have been singing in church since I was three.

It was part of who I was. But not anymore. I am going to become someone else. I am going to be the master of my fate. I am determined to make a good life for myself, by myself!

I am thankful as a divorcee. Marrying Bill was not a mistake I don't regret it. I learned a lot about myself and about life, and I have 2 amazing children. You have a choice, choose peace.

I worked part-time job as a cocktail waitress at a pool hall down the road from the house. I quickly procured a job at Lady Gold's Gym and got more shifts at the bar, even made upshifts and created more jobs for myself. If a cocktail shift wasn't open, I would make jello shots at home and come and sell them; yes, I know now that is called bootlegging; back then, it wasn't a big deal. I also became a promo model for Miller Lite and Bacardi. The funny thing is I didn't like the taste of either of them.

Working in a bar exposed the underbelly of town. Drugs were a big thing; all kinds being passed around in the bar. I started doing ecstasy. My parents watched both babies down the road. I am now a single mom-to-be. The bar was slow; someone handed me a pill. It was ecstasy. I took it, and things were feeling great and fuzzy. All of a sudden, my dad comes in and tells me Christian had disappeared.

My toddler had figured out how to open the front door! Now he was wandering the apartment complex at night, in DALLAS, where people disappear all the time. Immediately the E turned against me. My stomach was in knots; it felt like I had been gutted with a dull knife.

I was the FFA in high school. One day I went out to check on my show lamb. She was lying on the ground, barely breathing. A couple of rottweilers who had been missing from the neighbors house for a few days had chewed through the fence and ate her. Her whole stomach was opened up. Dad got his gun and ended her suffering. I cried so hard that day, and I'll never forget what her stomach looked like.

My stomach feels like hers looked when they said Christian was missing. I looked at them. I was getting sick, and they needed to take me with them; they looked at me and could tell I was in no shape to be entering a police station.

A neighbor called the police and reported a little boy walking around the apartment complex, so she took him in and fed him cookies. By the time my parents got home, he had been found.

That night I swore off ever doing drugs again.

New shift, a new focus on life. A man walked into the bar, a Frenchmen.

He was soft-spoken…" can I have your number he asked?" he looks like a nice guy; his eyes were gentle.

I looked back at my tray of jello shots, put them on the bar, and grabbed a napkin and pen to write my number down. I handed it to him. "I'm just recently separated from and getting a divorce." I am really busy, but you can call if you want.

I started modeling more and more. I worked non-stop, job to job every day. I started feeling so much more confident. Looking back, however, I was treading water, doing a lot, and getting nowhere.

I tried to get this divorce finalized as fast as possible. I hired a lawyer I met at the bar I served him a few times then hired him to help me. He was a bad lawyer who exploited me and my situation. He took advantage of my naivety and desperation.

On my way to work the next day I totaled my car by running into a trailer at a stop light. The airbag left burns on my forearms, but that was it; I was in a hurry to get to my shift. The good news was my insurance covered it and I was able to get a new car, one in my own name. The first one in my name. I was really proud of myself. It was a feather in my cap, I finally did something all on my own.

I was getting ready for a Miller Lite promo when the Frenchmen from the bar called. It had been a month, so I didn't recognize his voice.

He apologized for taking a long time to call. He was trying to put space between him and my recent breakup. I agreed to a one-hour dinner before my shift.

He was a gentleman; he picked me up and did all the right things. He seemed to care about me in a way I had never experienced before.

The more time I spent with him, the more I liked him. He didn't mind my crazy life and schedule; he was happy to help and take whatever time I had available.

Dirty Dancing

I had been paying the bills and saving money for a new washer and dryer, I had $1600 in cash, and I was going to pick out a set the next day when on my way to work, I put my planner on top of the car with all the money inside and pulled away, once I realized what I had done I searched up and down the street with a flashlight, I found nothing. It was gone. Back to zero. This was a huge setback in my new life.

It's funny how when you are in a storm and your mind ain't right, you get all kinds of unsolicited advice. A woman came in and sat down at the bar for an afternoon drink. She was young, skinny, and well-dressed. She and I talked, and she tipped big. The next time she came in, it was the same scenario. We talked, she drank, and the tip was huge!

One afternoon she comes in, and the rest of the bar is emptier than usual. She tells me that I am wasting my time working in such a slump. "you can make in one night what you make here in a week" where is this magical place? I asked…where do you work? A strip club, she said. "I can't. I just had a baby, and I don't think that is for me," she said, "not as a stripper as a cocktail waitress." Wow, I never thought about that. What an upgrade, I thought. I had just scrimped, saved, and pulled doubles to get the money for a new washer and dryer and lost it all! The possibility of being able to get It back so fast was enticing.

We lived in the Dallas metroplex there were several strip clubs. Of course, I was interested. I didn't want to waste my time cutting up limes and lemons and flirting with random dudes just to get a $5 tip. It was hard enough to be away from my babies. At least at night, they never knew I was gone, and I would only have to work weekends with that much money coming in.

I was desperate and picking up day bar shifts for a measly $80! This was a crappy job! I wanted out! Money was the answer to my problems. I am sold! The next day I went to find a new job.

I found the fanciest club in the area. Rumor had it that celebs and athletes were regulars. I wore black slacks and a white button-down dress shirt with a ruffled collar. A man wearing a suit came and sat with me as I was filling out the application.

He was about 6'2, with thin blonde hair and a round belly. I explained my work background and my financial situation. I think he could tell I was desperate. I think he preyed on the weak. I needed money and a lot of it quickly. He told me that the waitresses don't make as much as the entertainers do, and right now, there are no waitressing positions open.

He described nights when several girls went home with two thousand each. He reassured me that no one was allowed to touch the dancers, that the ladies were respected, and that they could come and go as they pleased, with no schedule, time clock, or shift duties.

He said I had an innocent look that would help me make more than other girls. He asked if I had any tattoos or piercings. I said no. Usually, he has dancers strip down and audition, but he would skip that for me. I thought I was lucky…Your hired, get yourself an outfit in the boutique, you can pay for it later and get started when you're ready.

I titled this book Diamond Girl for a very special reason. My mother, 2008ish, started a charity fundraiser for single moms called Diamond Girls. She has a heart for women who are raising kids by themselves. After watching me and seeing how impossible it was for me to support my children financially and give them a great life and still be available to raise them without any help from a man is darn near impossible when you don't have a great career or proper education. My mom had it in her heart to reach out and help any single mom, whether it be with money, clothes, babysitting, or just encouraging words and prayer.

I am the first one in her collection of Diamonds.

My mom has come to my rescue so many times. One holiday all of us grandkids were watching a movie in the side room at my grandparents' house.

I don't remember the movie we were all supposed to be watching, but I do remember an extended male family member who was young enough to be my older cousin called me over to sit on his lap. He said that he was the dad and I was the mom. I didn't want to sit on his lap, so I just sat on one of his knees as I was trying not to feel awkward as he, little by little, wrapped his hand around my waist and slipped a few fingers down the front of my jumper.

If you aren't aware, a jumper was like overalls but made of cloth. I was numb. I couldn't move; I was dumbstruck. Help is what I wanted to say. His hand wasn't there for maybe a minute, but it seemed like an eternity.

My mom pushed open the door, saw all the kids on the floor and then us on the couch, and said sternly, "Deanna come here," as she glared at him, I jumped up and ran past her out the door. I never wanted that to happen again to me or to any kid.

My mom was the hero. She would go on to save me again and again. Having parental instincts is truly a gift. I am so glad my parents follow their guts. Or what they give credit to as the Holy Spirit. The Bible says that the Father left the Holy Spirit for us to be able to receive messages sent from God. The Holy Spirit is an advocate that comes alongside us to help us.

DIVE DEEP

WHO WOULD YOU SAY IS YOUR HERO? WHY?

Prayer

Thank you, Jesus, that you sent your Spirit to help me. I need your voice in every area of my life. Help me to recognize you more and more. Speak to me about my children. Speak to me about everything. I am listening.

Amen

Parental Instincts

I didn't have the nerve to tell them the truth about my new job as an exotic dancer. I had bought a hairpiece to give myself a full mane of locks and to also help disguise my regular look. I bought a thong, a slip and a clear pair of high heels, not too high because I was afraid, I would fall. I got ready in the dressing room.

The girls just walked around naked; it was the first time I had seen anything other than my own stuff up close. All these girls were beautiful in their own individual way and had a confidence that I admired.

A tall brunette woman much older than me had a condo, a kid who was 8, and she drove a BMW. She seemed to have made a career out of this. She took me under her wing. This was her profession. She didn't fit the doped-up, desperate stereotype.

"The first thing you have to do once you are ready to start is to visit the DJ," she coached. He is in charge of your songs, and you have to go on his stage first, then the other two consecutive stages, one being in the VIP room. Once you complete all three, you are allowed to work the floor.

On special circumstances, if a guy wants you to get off the stage and come to his table and doesn't want to have to wait for you to complete the stage tour, then he can buy you off of the rotation then you need to tip the DJ to allow you to skip" she said all this as I was getting ready. "Thanks", I said "I appreciated your help."

"Hi, I'm Deanna," I said to DJ. He looked me up and down and grinned "this is your first time?" "Yes" why was he looking at me like that? It made me feel 12 years old and stupid, "you will be fine" he said. Just don't lock your knees. You may pass out." "Wow," I thought, "does my face look scared? I am not going to make money looking afraid, toughen up," I thought. "You didn't come this far for nothing."

He gave me the rundown, if I wanted a specific song played for my performance, he could do it, but it was an extra tip. I hope I walk out of here with enough money after tipping all these people, I said to myself.

He asked me if Deanna was my real name. Of course, I said. You need a stage name. That hadn't occurred to me at all. He continued, "not something stupid like a candy cane. This is a classy place. We want the customers to think it's your real name. Ok, uh, I don't know, I was drawing a blank. I hadn't thought about this. I felt rushed to make a decision and wanted to answer confidently to convince him I wasn't scared and that I was someone to be taken seriously. Olivia, I said. Why did I say that name? It was the first name that came to mind. It was the name my mom was going to give my little brother Nathaniel if he had been a girl.

"O, O, Olivia, to the stage." Ugh I feel like I just shat on my mom's baby's name. Puke! Here I go! Up the two stairs in the dressing room, past the mirror on the left for a final check of my outfit and hair.

I went into a blacked-out 5x5 box where there was a plexiglass window, and the DJ was on the other side giving me a thumbs-up. I took a left and faced the thick velvet curtain. On the other side of this curtain was the runway. DJ asked me for a song, 2 actually, which I flat out said, "I have no idea." I can't make any more decisions right now, I don't know any stripper songs, and if I did, I would have to pay him more! You pick I replied.

One performance on stage number one clothes on. Not too bad, everyone was staring, but I just walked back and forth like a slow supermodel. The second song was going to be the hardest. I went back behind the curtain to take off my slip (you aren't allowed to undress on stage in front of the crowd because it was a "classy" place"). One song left only a few minutes, and it's over, I thought. Man, I was thankful for all this extra hair!!

I walked through the curtain; the spotlight was blinding. I stood there stunned. What do I do now? The song rang out with lyrics "wake me up inside." I turned around to leave, and DJ shook his head. M O O V E, he mouthed. I started moving, with my back to the crowd. The rules were no touching your private parts ". It was a "classy place." I got a new definition of the word "classy" that night.

The lyrics to the song rang out so loud, it was speaking to me. Music was always a place I could melt into and be moved or changed, or inspired. This was the same but different: *"How can you see into my eyes Like open doors? Lading you down into my core, Where I've become so numb. Without a soul, My Spirit's sleeping somewhere cold, Until you find it there and lead it back Home. (Wake me up) Wake me up inside. (I can't wake up) Wake me up inside. (Save me) Call my name and save me from the dark. (Wake me up) Bid my blood to run. (I can't wake up) Before I come undone. (Save me) Save me from the nothing I've become. Now that I know what I'm without, You can't just leave me. Breathe into me and make me real. Bring me to life.*

I turned my back to whoever was watching so they wouldn't see the tears in my eyes. I wanted to run. I wanted to be saved right there right then, but again like everything else so far in my life. I told myself it's too late for that. I was alone.

A few more stages, a few more songs. More music that spoke to me to get out of there and never come back. One of them was playing louder and harder. The words to the song rang in my ears, piercing my soul. It said stuff like "break the faith, a fall from grace, know my faults, see my loss, hear my cries, hear my cries, lend me your ears, come with me."

I have fallen so far from grace. I didn't want to be here. I hushed my Spirit and succumbed to the environment.

I used those words to help me dance and pull whoever was watching into the mess I was in and the disgust I felt. Broken and lost was working in my favor in this place. Money started appearing on the stage. The lights were moving. I couldn't see faces.

There were a few different times that when I looked down, there was someone there waiting to hand money to me…I let them but didn't look them in the eyes. Not sure why these guys wanted to give me money. I didn't feel sexy. I was 23 years old crying on stage. It's the implants. That is why you are making money, I told myself. My legs were shaking, and my fingers were ice cold, but inside I was going numb.

As soon as I was done, I grabbed my things and ran for the dressing room. I looked into the mirror, thinking something about me was different, but I looked exactly the same. I was ok. Nothing had changed on the outside anyway. No one would be able to notice from looking at me that I was torn inside.

I put my slip on and walked out to sit at the middle main room bar with my back to the front door. I sat there and tried to breathe and compose myself, the next step was getting someone to ask me for a dance, or maybe I needed to ask them.

As I sat there going through my options and rehearsing what I was going to say. A whisper in my ear said, "D, don't turn around. Your dad just walked in! He is at the door."

What in the world! Is this a cruel joke, I thought my dad would never come to a place like this. I knew the voice warning me. It was the door guy. His job is to be on the floor for any, and all customer needs.

He lived in the same apartment complex as my parents. In pure panic, I ducked under the bar, crawled all the way around on my hands and knees back to the VIP room, and ran upstairs to hide. I peered over the balcony in the darkest corner to see if he was really there. My heart was beating out of my chest. What was he doing here?

How could my dad have known this was where I would be? The door to VIP opened, and in stepped my dad! I saw him look around. He was looking for me. I could tell by the way he scoured the place. Oh, please don't come upstairs. I was trapped! He stopped, turned around, and left.

I couldn't work after that. I went to the dressing room and got ready to go home. On the drive back, I decided I would go straight to mom and accuse dad of being at a strip club. That is exactly what I did. I marched right into her house and said, "mom, did you know dad was at a strip club tonight!" I was hoping to flip the heat onto him instead of me. She looked right into my eyes and said so calmly, "yes, he has been looking for you. He went to several to find you." An immense amount of guilt flooded my body.

How would he know to look there, I asked? "he had a feeling," she said. I was so embarrassed. Dad then came home, I confessed, and he asked me how long I had been working there. He requested that if I was going to work there that he would pick me up so that he could keep me safe. I crawled into bed with my two little angels and fell asleep.

This was it. This is my decided occupation, and it won't be forever it'll just be until I am financially back on my own two feet. Therefore, I am going to be the best, and I am going to take all money I can. No more dignity or pride; from now on I am putting myself first.

This job was fake. It was a masquerade. I enjoyed the separateness from real life that it offered. I can be hard and selfish, use a false identity, and make money. It was an alternative reality where I could escape and pretend.

Over a short time, this mask, my Olivia mask, was savvy, resourceful, prideful, and self-centered, greedy. My heart, the true me, grew colder and darker with each passing night.

I walked by the bartender, and he slid over a shot and said you look like you need this. I looked around to see if anyone was looking and drank down that shot as fast as I could...ugh, it was awful!

The liquid courage kicked in, and the next song and stage performance went by fast, back to the front for one more song on the side stage. Alcohol became as necessary as false lashes.

DIVE DEEP

WHEN YOU ARE STRESSED, WHAT DO YOU REACH FOR? DO YOU HAVE ANY VICES THAT YOU MAY REBOUND TO IN DESPERATE TIMES? SHOPPING, SUBSTANCES, FOOD ETC?

_____
_____
_____
_____
_____
_____
_____

Single Mom Status

There were happy days with the kids at the apartment pool. I loved watching them play with each other. Christian and Victoria are perfect little bundles of joy. Christian is funny. He loves making people laugh. He is more cautious than Tori. He wouldn't jump into the water without grabbing my hands first.

Victoria is an outgoing tiny little thing. She has no fear. I had to watch her closely because she would jump in the pool without me even knowing that she was ready. "Let go. I can do it myself" was her favorite thing to say. They are so opposite but so close to each other. I am glad I had them close in age so that they can always be best friends. If anything ever happens to me, they will have each other.

I look at them now in awe of their resilience in life. Christian is so handsome and intelligent. He is my Navy Sailor, and more than that, he loves God with all his heart. I pray that his wife is the perfect, God-fearing, generous and kind person that compliments him and brings out the best in him. Victoria is shopping for prom and planning her big move to Flagstaff in the summer. She is drop-dead gorgeous with a fiery spirit like her Mimi.

I can't wait to see what she does and who she chooses as her forever person. I pray she marries a man who loves God and is generous and kind, tall and athletic.

Jared, her daddy, is going to have a hard time giving her away. That man thinks she is the most precious thing on the planet. An ironic fact: Jared's mom's name is Victoria, and he always wanted his firstborn son to be named Christian. How cool is that? To think God worked everything out so beautifully for us all.

Back to the past: 23yrs old, still trying to get a divorce. I moved out of the house we bought the kids, and I moved in with my parents. I couldn't afford it. I wanted to live with my parents until I got my own place that I could afford.

Never ask if the guy wants a dance. Just walk up, smile and, say hi, start a conversation. Then once you have him talking to you, he asks you to take a seat at his table. If he doesn't, then you initiate it by saying can I sit down, or do you want company. Wait for a new song to come on and give him a dance. He buys another dance from you after he gets you a drink. Inviting more girls over starts the party.

The more time you spend at one table, the more it increases your chance of making good money, and you are the one in control. This customer can count on you to make sure he has a good time, and the next time he comes in, he will ask for you again.

I started to make a lot of money. In fact, purse loads of it. The problem was I was drinking more and more every night.

I had met someone who I started talking to before I began working as a stripper. He was a Frenchman who had been taking me to and from work, so my dad didn't have to.

Frenchy kept me safe and proposed to my parents to take me away for a few days. We flew to Lake Tahoe during the spring. It is such a cute town, and we got to know each other so much better on that trip. I fell for him that weekend.

Growing up, I used to put on talent shows for my parents. I would sing, Landon would tell jokes, and Stephen would dance. There is one home video of me singing, "I want money, lots and lots of money" lol…how true that was, and now that I had a job to get me lots of crazy cash, I quit all my other jobs and started acting like a diva. The frenchman took me shopping in Tahoe and bought me many ridiculous items. It made me feel like I was going to be well taken care of by him. I had never experienced this kind of relationship.

He was a romantic and spoiled me beyond his means which ended up being something he resented me for towards the end. At the time he was gentle and kind.

We went to church together. This was a big deal for me, that he would go and participate. Most of all he loved my kids. He met all my family, and they welcomed him with open arms. They liked us together. I had never brought anyone home other than Bill, and he wasn't ever accepted like Frenchy was.

I was happy, I was making so much money. I felt like I had made a good life. I knew in the back of my mind that this job wouldn't last much longer. The closer I got to frenchy, the guiltier I felt for working as a stripper.

I started drinking more and more until one night. I lost a lot of money. I was wasted. One of the girls backstage saw what a mess I was and gave me a bump of cocaine. "This is gonna get you fixed, honey. Snort it" she rolled up a bill from her clutch and handed it to me. It sobered me up instantly. I looked at myself in the mirror, I was fine, but I looked different. She gave me a little more to take home.

When Frenchy picked me up, I said, "look what one of the girls gave me," I handed him the bag, and he looked at it and then at me with a terrifying stare. I confessed what had happened. He pulled out a scale from his closet at home that he said he uses for weed and weighed it. "A significant amount he said" we finished it off together and stayed up all night.

Stages and spotlights are familiar territories. In high school, I would travel and sing country songs with the FFA talent team. I loved being up there and putting on a great show, and bringing home the wins. Our team went to state every year, and we won state and went to Nationals my Junior year. I wore white Rockies, red boots, and a sequence red, white, and blue vest it was so much fun.

High School was good for me. I loved being in a small town in east Texas. I loved playing sports; my parents made me try everything to see what I liked. My dad took time to umpire at my softball games, practice playing tennis with me, and even spotted me while I learned the back handspring for cheer. Cheering was my favorite; everyone came to the football games. It was like a town party every Friday night or at least at the home games.

DIVE DEEP
SHARE/REMEMBER A GOOD CHILDHOOD MEMORY, ONE THAT MAKES YOU FEEL YOUNG AGAIN.

_____
_____
_____
_____
_____
_____
_____

Exploited

Dancing started to get easy. I could put on a show and get paid to do it. I figured out how to be two different people. Olivia really liked doing coke. She was a fun, young, dumb, sweet Texas girl who could laugh at any of the stupidest jokes. I was completely numb from the inside out, and I could drink like a fish and keep all the money I had made.

I bought a new SUV. I remember when I was car shopping, I told them straight up what I did for a living, and they let me take home a brand-new Cadillac Escalade for the week to see if I liked it. I wasn't surprised that they let me take it home. I had gotten accustomed to men just giving me stuff. I had a flow of "regular" customers.

I walked into the apartment complex across the street from my parents and put a deposit and the first month's rent down. It was a cute two-bed two baths with vaulted ceilings. I hired a personal trainer. I thought I was finally thriving. I have done it! I have achieved all the things I set out to have.

One night, no different from the rest. I was asked to dance in VIP for a pro football player and his chiropractor. I thought, SCORE! I loved being asked to join a big fish at his party.

It will be all the business I need tonight. I have seen girls bring other girls with them to VIP. I assumed it was because they were kinky or bisexual. Why would you want to split the cash with another girl? If you can just handle it yourself, you can go home richer.

Now I know why, while I was entertaining the humungous football player, he unbuttoned his pants. Ewe gross, what was he thinking, I looked around for security, and of course, upstairs, there wasn't any. Then it hit me, now I know why you don't go upstairs to VIP alone. I didn't know how to handle him. If I make him feel bad, he may not pay me. I went with it and acted like it was fine. Grossest dance ever! His chiropractor was a big guy too and wanted to adjust my back, so like the idiot I was and greedy for money, I let him. I laid down on the floor on my stomach in VIP to let him crack my spine. I couldn't wait to escape their company.

The longer you stick it out, the more money you make, so I held in there as long as possible, ordering food, drinking, and playing pool with them. It was the roughest money I ever made. I degraded myself and had become a very sad girl.

There was one regular that thought he was my boyfriend. He didn't want me to dance for him. He wanted a friend, so I became a friend. After several evenings with me, I knew his whole life story, his marriage, kids, divorce, and business, and he paid for my time sitting talking eating and drinking.

Eventually, to keep up the act, I told him my real name, about my kids, and my divorce (I left out the part about my boyfriend). I needed two more of these customers a week, and I would be set. I took full advantage of this short-round middle-aged man. I would lie and make up stories to get him to pay me more. It was pathetic.

I lost all respect for men. They were all so weak. I enjoyed feeling like the one with all the power. Looking back, it was a false sense of power, a warped reality.

One night I had just finished the stage routine, I walked around the stage and noticed all of the guys from the old bar I used to work at sitting there. I still remember the humiliating feeling that came over me. A little more of my self-esteem died when they recognized me, and then I had to sit and talk to them.

I pretended to be happy and rich and loving life. They didn't ask for dances. I never saw them again after that. Word was getting around to more and more people. Being a dancer wasn't a secret anymore.

My divorce lawyer showed up and said he wanted payment. I danced for him and asked if we were even, "not quite," he said, "come to my office tomorrow, and we can work something out." I knew what that meant, and I didn't want to pay him. He hadn't helped me at all yet and it would set me back if I did.

I went to his office downtown and got it over with. ... I was already empty of any self-respect, but I was at a new low.

On the way home, I was racing down the freeway illegally over the limit and wanted to just turn the wheel, off of the road. How nice it would be to just be done with it all and be at peace. This was the first time I let in the thoughts of suicide and it wouldn't be the last.

Little did I know that the divorce documents would be rejected by the judge. What a waste of my time! This was when rage began to form in my heart. It callused me and pushed me even further into darkness.

Bill was required to pay child support even though I didn't request it. Texas law is or was; unless the father of the children is incarcerated, he must pay support. Will I ever have a chance to start over? Bill and I through mediation decided that he would get all money, cards, house etc and I would keep the kids. This made us both happy. It would take seven years and a move to the great state of Arizona for this agreement to be legally finalized.

DIVE DEEP

WHEN HAVE YOU BEEN BETWEEN A ROCK AND A HARD PLACE? DID IT RENDER YOU HOPELESS? OR DID IT DRIVE YOU TO FIGHT YOUR WAY OUT?

_____
_____
_____
_____
_____
_____
_____

Hmmm...I Can't Remember

My relationship with Frenchie turned toxic when we started doing drugs together. He would have more control over them than I could. I just couldn't stop wanting more. I loved feeling numb to any emotion and I could fake my happiness. I felt it was the only thing keeping me alive, the only thing I had to get me through a day, the only thing I wanted.

I started to need more and more money to support my habit. I worked more nights and even some days. As I began spending more time at the club, Frenchie started drifting away from me and spending more time with a group of people that didn't respect me at all.

I was hardly ever invited to what they were doing or anywhere they went. I didn't care; I didn't blame them, it hurt my feelings, but they never knew the real me. To them I was the stripper with two kids. The thought that no one ever really wanted me after Bill, was confirmed in my mind. I am undesirable. I am not wanted. I am a loser.

Drugged Or What?

I went into the club, got ready, and came out to see only a few patrons there for afternoon cocktails. One man I recognized as a "regular," not a regular in the sense that he was a baller. He actually rarely ever bought a dance from anyone he was just a looker.

He was a small framed man with salt and pepper hair. Everyone knew that if you sat with him, it was simply for a drink and conversation. Sometimes if you wanted to stay longer, he would bring out a deck of cards to play a game of some kind, and if you did, he would pay you for your time. I thought, "why not? There isn't anyone else in here that has any money" I had learned how to read the room. I could tell if they were lookers or spenders.

I sat down with Mr. cards at the bar, and he ordered me a drink. The conversation, from what I remember, was boring. He wasn't funny or interesting at all. We played one game, and I was ready to get out of there. Once my drink was gone, he gave me a few 20-dollar bills.

I decided the day was done. I didn't want to be there anymore. I changed out of my clothes, said goodbye to the doorman, and woke up in the hospital. A police officer was standing beside my hospital bed. The room was grey and blue. My eyes were blurry and fuzzy, but I could make out my mom. She was there. How embracing I thought.

How did I get here, I wondered? My face hurt, and my head was pounding. I looked down and saw a boot on my left foot. "Who was driving?" the officer asked. "I was," I tried to say, but my mouth wouldn't open. I was wired shut. I knew I had broken my jaw. Dang it, this was the second time that my jaw was broken in a car accident.

When I was 12, me, my mom and my new baby brother Nathaniel hit a patch of black ice going home from church late one night in December. The last thing I said to my mom was to be careful because it was Friday the 13th.

She told me to lie down and go to sleep and that we didn't believe in those kinds of things. I took my seat belt off, which probably saved my life because the car rolled several times. I woke up in the hospital with a broken jaw and a major concussion; my head was the size of a watermelon and a broken collar bone.

To make matters worse, I had flown out of the car into a snowbank full of poison oak. I was covered with red itchy bumps. Turns out my mom saved me then too. With a broken neck, she carried her baby, my little brother Nathaniel to a house and handed him off to the people inside.

Her head had to be held up by her hand, clenching a fist full of hair to the sky. She went back out in the dark, in the snow, to look for me. You were turning blue, she said, she found me in the ditch, laid down beside me and held me until the ambulance arrived.

She was almost paralyzed for the rest of her life, but the fervent prayers of our church and my father went straight to heaven, and God sent his angels to save her. Now she is healthier than most women her age and has all the physical abilities of anyone else. I healed up just fine too.

Now here I am with my jaw broken for the second time. The officer replied, "no, ma'am, when we found you, you had gone through the windshield on the passenger's side." "no one was driving me," I winced in pain as I tried to talk, "I promise, it was just me." He continued to insist I was covering for someone. I really thought I had driven home. I was confused.

I had a vague glimpse, just a flash of a memory that I kept replaying, trying to dig deeper for more information, but it was just all the same; I was driving, it was dark, I passed the exit on the freeway. My car swerved into the right lane and I corrected too hard to the left, pulling my body right. Then my heart-racing, eyes bulge then I see my car head for a solid concrete median, then nothing. Each time replay made me sweat and my heart race, but nothing else ever came back to me. Not being found, not being rushed to the hospital, no one else with me, nothing…. The cop told me when I was ready to tell him the truth. He would be happy to take my statement. It was frustrating to hear that they thought I lied. I was frustrated.

They never took my blood alcohol levels or drug tested me. I wish they had because I had been clean for a few days, and I think I was drugged by Mr. Cards.

The officer left, he thought I was either covering for someone or lying. I was in and out of consciousness for a couple of days. When I finally was able to go to the bathroom on my own. I noticed my face was different. They had to put a metal plate in my jaw. One side of my face wasn't even, one side was bigger than the other, and that is the way it will be forever. I am permanently ugly… way to go, dummy, I said to myself.

To this day, I don't have any memory of what happened after I left the club that late afternoon. I surmise that there was something in that drink that compromised me. I promised myself never to do day shifts again.

Betrayal

I noticed I was getting bigger. Can it be? Oh no! I was pregnant. I could feel it. Frenchie brought over a test, and sure enough, we were going to have a baby. I was still in crutches. We didn't know what to think or say. Should I be excited? After all, I do love him. We called my parents over to my place to talk. My dad made a comment that I am not able to handle the two kids I already had, much less another.

My dad told Frenchie about the time I passed out. Christian needed his diaper changed, so he changed it himself and decorated all the walls with his poo. I was embarrassed. Now it's real mom, dad, and Frenchie all know I am a loser. A horrible mom.

Dad was right. I couldn't handle what I already had. How could I take on another baby? Frenchie and I cried after my parents left. We cried about the choices as we talked about terminating the pregnancy.

A few days went by, maybe a week, but still, we didn't know what we were going to do. I went to work, but I was so stressed, something didn't feel right anymore, but I also wasn't high. The realness of life was heavy. Being on cocaine numbed reality, and now the floodgates of pint up emotions came pouring out. I called Frenchie, but he wouldn't answer.

Hours later, he finally picked up and explained that he was out with his mom at a bar.

That is super weird because his mom isn't the late-night bar type. I decided to drive myself home in the truck he had given me since I had totaled my car.

Something was up. I could feel it. I went home to my apartment and kept calling him but to no avail. I stayed up till 3 am. This kind of feeling was familiar; I had been cheated on before.

I decided to call his mom. I needed to at least know he was ok and maybe passed out on her couch. She told me she hadn't seen him at all that night. Right after I hung up with her, he called and told me straight up that he had cheated on me. My stomach dropped. Why did I think this guy was different? Why did I let him into my life? Why did I introduce him to my amazing babies? Why would I want to have another one with him? I am such a fool.

I decided not to let him come to the apartment. I met him in the IHOP parking lot. I got out of the truck screaming, and I could feel the stress in my body, and I kept thinking about how unhealthy this was for the little one inside me. I yelled at him with tears streaming down my face that I was done! "You are just like Bill. I hate you, I hate what you did, I want nothing to do with you, and I am having this baby without you."

He was crying, too. He felt terrible for what he did and knew that it was wrong. He said he knew it was the one thing that I wouldn't tolerate, and he was trying to get rid of me because he was scared.

Cheating was the one way he knew he could get rid of me because I would break up with him instead of him having to break it off with me.

When he said that, my heart, what was left of it, literally crumbled. I had never felt so unraveled in my life. I felt so abandoned. I got in the truck and went home.

I took all of the stuff that was his and put it outside, locked the door, and cried myself to sleep. He showed up in the morning to get the truck from me, and I went nuts on him. I wanted to scratch his eyes out. I kept throwing the keys, making it impossible for him to leave. I would calm down and let him get close, then start pounding on him. I was so irate he had to call my dad to come over and hold me down.

Over the next month, I kept dancing, trying to figure out my next move. I was so sad, so lost. I looked forward to the moments I could finally melt into the music and feel good while I was entertaining; then a customer would say something stupid that I absolutely hated, like, "you don't belong here, or your too good for this place, or tell me about yourself?" That made me so mad! I didn't want to tell them anything. I despised what I had to do for money. I was disgusted by men.

DIVE DEEP

THINK ABOUT A TIME WHEN YOU WERE LET DOWN BY SOMEONE. HOW DID IT MAKE YOU FEEL? HOW HAVE YOU PROCESSED IT SINCE THEN?

_____
_____
_____
_____
_____
_____
_____

1 Peter 5:8

Be alert and of sober mind. Your enemy, the devil, prowls around like a roaring lion looking for someone to devour.

The Darkest Hour

Frenchie began calling and sending over gifts. He said he missed the kids. He worked his way back, and we stayed together. He was sincere and repentant, so much so that I truly believed that he would never do that to me again. We went to see a doctor for an ultrasound. It was a boy, and it looked like the drugs I had done before hadn't hurt the baby, as far as the doctor could tell. We chose not to terminate.

Covenant Church in Carrollton, Texas, has been good to us. My parents moved all of us kids to this town right after I graduated high school. Mom and dad both got jobs at the church's private school called AHA, and my brothers had the opportunity to go there. I have a great memory the first time the Pastor's family took us to lunch. It was September 15th, my 18th birthday.

We were in the front lobby waiting for a table when Pastor took out a one-hundred-dollar bill from his billfold, turned to me, and said, "I heard it's your birthday today?" "yes, I'm 18 I replied" he held out the money for me to take. I shook my head, "oh, no, I can't take that" his son shouted who was 15 shouted, "if you don't take it, I will."

Pastor pushed the money my way again, and I took it from him and said thank you so much! I had never gotten that much money given to me before. This guy was a tall, regal-looking southern pastor and author. Why would he want to give me money? I thought maybe he sees something great in me. Ever since then, I knew I was welcome at his church no matter what happened.

Even though I had no self-esteem, I knew I would be welcome at Covenant Church Dallas after all the lead pastor met me at 18 and invested in me. It was a small investment that kept me feeling like no matter what happens I can always go to church.

The kids and I went to service together. Sometimes Frenchie went with us. Maybe this is going to be a new start. It had been a long time since I had been to church. They had a prayer line created in the front, right at the foot of the stage. Pastors, elders, and leaders of the church stood on either side and if you want prayer, you could walk through the line and let them pray over you.

I was nervous but decided to walk through the line. I was wearing regular clothes, a t-shirt, and baggy overalls. I thought I was hiding my baby bump.

I walked slowly through the train of prayer warriors, my head stayed down, and I continued to just walk when right at the end of the line was a woman who was a Pastor. She reached out her hand, put it on my stomach, and prayed for my baby. I stopped walking and covered my face with my hands, and wept.

How did she know, I thought? As she prayed, I asked God to take this baby from me, that I wanted to terminate it, and that I wanted the baby to be with Him, not with me. I am a loser. I am unwanted. I am ill-equipped; I am a horrible mother. I can't do this.

One night, Frenchie insisted on staying with me at work. I did my stage work, then picked up a lone ranger at a table between the stage and the bar that Frenchie was sitting at. I did the usual. I sat down beside the customer and had a brief conversation. When the next song came on, I started giving him a lap dance. Frenchie had never seen me "in action." Halfway into the song, I looked up and saw him standing at the bar facing me, holding a glass in one hand. His body was frozen. I made eye contact with him and saw tears rolling down his cheeks.

I stopped moving. I don't like to call it dancing. Dancing is an art and what I was doing was not art to me. "I am so sorry; I have to go," I said to the customer, who was clueless as to what was happening and had no response. I grabbed my stuff and walked over to the bar. He whispered, "I am sorry, I can't do this. I never want you to do this ever again," I nodded my head and told him it was over. Then, I will quit. We left the club together.

We continued to talk more about the baby and how it is probably better if we terminated. He lived with his brother; I was soon to be homeless because I had no work; financially, it was so irresponsible to bring another life into this world.

We drove to an abortion clinic. It looked so run down and dirty. It was in the back ally of some ghetto apartments. It felt wrong, so we left.

However, when the weekend came, and we talked about it some more, we just wanted life to go back to drinking and partying, so we did exactly that. I did drugs, and it made me disgusted with myself for doing drugs while pregnant, but I justified it because I was going to end the pregnancy soon, and I didn't want to face any reality, and cocaine took all reality away from me.

Another clinic the next week. It was cleaner and on a good street, but It had protestors outside; they put us both on edge, so we left and, that next weekend, did more drugs.

We both knew we had to end it soon before it was too late. In my mind, I thought that once I terminated, then I could get my life back on track. The next abortion clinic we went to was the cleanest, and there were no protesters in sight. It was in a decent neighborhood.

We went inside. It was a dimly lit, small dark front desk. There was one counter with a young girl sitting behind the desk, who stood as we walked in. I couldn't find any words to speak to her as she said hello. Frenchie did all the talking. I wondered what she thought of us, of our situation, if I was being pressured into this because I wasn't talking. I signed some papers and sat in the waiting room to the right of the counter. It was just as dark. The walls were deep brown laminate walls. It was the saddest waiting room I had ever been in.

There were several other women waiting, some of them a man sat beside them. No one made eye contact with each other.

"Deanna," the nurse called. I stood and walked alone into a hallway and into a room. The floors were white square tile, but it didn't lighten the room up at all. The walls seemed even darker in here, and the only light was the swivel light over the bed. There was an examination bed like in the hospital and big swivel light over the bed. There wasn't any room for any more furniture in there other than the tall white metal locker.

The lady asked me to lay on the bed undressed from the waist down. She numbed me and walked out. I lay there, wondering if what I was doing was going to be the end of me. The final nail in my coffin. I was such a disgrace I couldn't bring another human into this world with me.

She came back in with a man in a white coat. He stuck what felt like a long sharp knife-like object inside me. It felt like he had cut something in my stomach.

I could feel it! I didn't think I would have to feel anything! It hurt so bad it made me shrill and I grabbed the sides of the bed. As the pain subsided, darkness crept over me.

I felt the darkest of darkness like I had never known before creeping through the cracks in the walls and door and ceiling into that room, and it floated over my bed and laid on me. I was the saddest I had ever been. I felt gone, empty, and hopeless.

They sent me home, home to bleed it out. I cried while I explained to Frenchmen what happened in the room. I also told him about the shadow that came into the room and was on me now. He took me straight to the ER. We ran inside. We wanted to see if we could reverse what had just happened. We were wrong. We knew it. This was a mistake. Why are we so selfish and stupid? We wanted to fix it and make it better?..But, It was too late. I killed my baby.

I went to my apartment. I sat in the bathroom and waited for the passing of life inside me. I watched as the blood from who I would have named Hayden pour out of me into the toilet. It was the last time I would cry for a very long time.

I don't want to live anymore. I am a waste of life. The feelings of worthlessness were so strong. I wanted more drugs right then; it was too painful to comprehend life and functioning. What a mess I was. I don't want this; I want to escape. I want to die. I did coke the rest of the week.

DIVE DEEP

IF YOU HAVE SUFFERED FROM THOUGHTS OF SUICIDE, NOW IS YOUR TIME TO HEAL. SHARING IS NOT SHAMEFUL; IT'S LIBERATING. SHARE WITH SOMEONE SO YOU CAN MOVE FORWARD IN FULL HEALTH.

_____
_____
_____
_____
_____
_____
_____

Psalm 139:12

Even the darkness is not dark to you; the night is bright as the day, for darkness is as light with you.

    The person I am today is night and day who I was then. I was a shell of a person unrecognizable to me now. How I wish I could talk to my 20 something self and give her a wake-up call, hope and another way. Abortion was what I chose to do after having two beautiful, healthy babies. Aborting my third pregnancy was the biggest mistake of my life.

Two kids with one man to whom I was still legally married and pregnant with another man's baby was a shame that I couldn't comprehend to bare. I had sold my soul, sold my body, and compromised myself in every way I had never imagined doing.

Immature and naive, I thought that I would not be able to live with the shame of multiple kids with different men. Little did I know that killing my baby was more shameful than the shame of what people thought of me for keeping him. Every day since the abortion, I have thought about my baby.

Years later, I still dream about him. My dreams get more frequent around his due date in May. I would give anything to do it over. I would keep him. I would love him. I could still move to Lake Havasu City, the city God called me to. I would still marry Jared, and we would have Benjamin. Family of 6 instead of 5. I would be much happier.

As I write this, there have been 61 million abortions. What a huge number. I can't even wrap my head around it. It's a small country full of humans who might have lived. One in every four women by the age of 40 will have an abortion.

So many kids, so many moms and dads, left with regret and wondering what might have been.

I see that there are many options and support systems in place to help women. The lie we, as women, have bought into and believe is that "it's my body it's my choice"

[19] Do you not know that your bodies are temples of the Holy Spirit, who is in you, whom you have received from God? You are not your own; [20] you were bought at a price. Therefore, honor God with your bodies. 1 Corinthians 6:19-20

How do we have doctors who have sworn an oath to "do no harm" ending a human life? I am not here to judge you if you feel different or if you have had an abortion. I cannot nor will I, throw a stone. However, having been down the road of pain and lived through the aftermath, please heed my words.

No matter the circumstances that lead to your pregnancy or the lifestyle you have. Hope is on the other side of choosing life over death. You can get through anything. Say yes to the challenge of carrying and delivering your baby, and there will be people who God will bring to you to help you figure out the rest.

But those who hope in the Lord
Will renew their strength.
They will soar on wings like eagles;
They will run and not grow weary,
They will walk and not be faint.

Fake Beginnings

Life seemingly was getting better. The kids and I move into Frenchie's house. We picked out a house to have built for us in a new development. Things started to resemble a normal life. I was interested in getting an education into a quick trade some sort. Something I could start making more than minimum wage in, something I could make my own schedule. I wanted to be a better mother; I was ready to face the world as a new person. I enrolled in the Paul Mitchell school of esthetics, it was a short program and I could make ladies feel pretty and have a flexible schedule that would work around raising kids. Frenchie flew me to New York, sparing no expense. We saw his sister, who was an aspiring actress in New York. She performed in a play. His mom and aunt came along too.

One night we were out on the town in the Big Apple, and he decided to leave me to go flirt with the bartender. I wasn't going to tolerate that at all. I left the bar and walked back to the hotel. He chased me all the way back trying to calm me down and explain.

I got to the hotel and started looking into flights to go home. "Look!" He said, "just look" I wouldn't look at him, so he put the box in my face. It was a beautiful ring with three stones, past, present, and future, set in a wide platinum band.

"I was going to propose to you! I was excited about it and was sharing my story with the woman at the bar, that is all! I love you. Will you marry me? I had the plan to take you around Central Park in a carriage but now it's all ruined, don't leave! Please! I love you!"

I felt so dumb. "Yes, I said, "I'm sorry." We made up, and I called my parents to tell them the good news. He had already asked their permission. My mom asked if I was ok, and she said my voice didn't sound happy. I couldn't tell her about the ridiculous fight we had just had. It would taint her memory of this moment that was supposed to be beautiful.

Gateway Drug

Back home on the weekends, I still had it in me to party. Coke wasn't available, but meth was, and it was cheaper, so we started snorting meth. It was so much stronger. I hooked right away; meth was my thing now. The lines were smaller, and the high lasted longer. I was more productive instead of drinking away the coke high and passing out. Meth breaks down differently in the body. It's like you are going a hundred miles an hour, so much energy and false clarity, no alcohol necessary.

Something about it was worse than coke. I knew it deep down but couldn't stop. At the time, I couldn't explain it, but I knew my brain was acting differently. I wasn't numb anymore. It was a high that made me more aware but distorted reality all at the same time. Meth opened the porn door in our relationship. Meth changes you.

I don't even know how it got introduced into our private life, but it did. I was so high that it didn't bother me at all. I had turned into the person I never thought I would be. A drug-addicted mother of two. The lingering regret that never went away and depression of all my choices. The darkness of the abortion, was always there looming in the corner, waiting to finish me off.

When you're a druggie you can spot a fellow addict. It was easy to spot who was like me and who I could use to get a hookup. Beauty school was no different than anywhere else.

Meth ran through so many hands in that place. I never ran out. It became the source of my energy.

I had no motivation or will to do anything until I did a line of meth. It had turned into an everyday addiction. Frenchie couldn't keep up with me. He would make attempts to get me to stop or slow down. I started getting and doing drugs without him.

We would fight all the time, and I continued to push him away more and more. Being on meth would make me snap for no reason. Anger was always right under the surface. Anything would and could set me into a tailspin. I would physically push him and scream in his face.

One time, when he wouldn't do something that I asked, not sure what it was, I just snapped. I started walking down the street, screaming at the top of my lungs about nonsense. He just stood in the doorway watching, I came back to yell at him more, and I would say things to get a reaction from him. He just laughed at me, which made me even angrier, I was going crazy, and he couldn't help me. He asked me to leave, so I packed up and left.

I moved back into my parent's apartment. I would sneak out for late-night visits with my frenchie, trying to convince him I was better and we could fix our relationship.

The decent, kind, loving person I was, or what little of me that was left, died when my baby died, and I know that Frenchie never forgave me for going through with the abortion. We were so broken, and being together made the reality of our brokenness more evident.

Trapped

I was walking to the end of the apartments and was waiting outside for a drug dealer when a man pulled up in a white Mercedes car. He wasn't anyone I knew. He rolled his window down and asked me what I was doing. "Nothing," I said. He asked me on a date, and I asked, "right now?" "Yeah!" He said. "OK," I replied and jumped into his car. I noticed him dust off white powder from the middle console as I got in. We went down the street to shoot pool at a bar. It was mid-day. I wasn't into him I was just bored and wanted a free drink.

Looking back, I can't believe how far from common sense it was. I had no regard or care for my life. I didn't care what happened to me, and I don't think anyone else cared either. What does it matter if I leave with a stranger, life is mute.

A cocktail waitress who I knew because this was the bar my Bill used to work at. She came up and whispered in my ear. "Do you know who that is?" "I think he said, ___, (keeping him annonomous)why?" I thought she was going to say his card was declined. He was driving a nice car but was wearing sweatpants and a dirty t-shirt. "That is ___ ___ of the Dallas Cowboys. Girl, last I checked, he was married," she said. "Crap," I thought, "what now… I don't want to be a homewrecker on top of everything else that I already am."

I left the bar immediately didn't even say anything to the man, I bummed a ride from a friend back to my apartment.

A New Job

DebtXS is a company my mom worked for that helps people consolidate and eliminate student loan debt. They hired me because of her influence. I was out of the reach of bad people, and there was no more going to bars and clubs. I had a normal job and a chance to start again.

I moved up to one of the top salespeople pretty quickly. I went from a cubicle to an office of my own. I liked working a desk job. I was making good money. I started buying myself real clothes from J. Crew. I was hanging out with businessmen and women.

But I was still miserably alone. Every second that I didn't have something to do, the dreadfulness of the reality of my broken heart would creep in. I kept meth readily available for when I would start to think about my awful existence.

I also loved going out at night and could be around other people who were just as bad as I was. I was delusional; I thought I could quit any time I wanted. I thought I could control it. Now I can see it had its tentacles in me.

I started dating again. I partied every weekend. Just abandoning my kids at my parents' house. My parents financially supported my kids. In the meantime, I made sure I had plenty of money to spend on drugs.

I threw myself an elaborate birthday party at a fancy hotel in downtown Dallas I was 23.

I bought myself a dress and filled the hotel with people, alcohol, and drugs. People who are "fake friends" are the kind of friends you only see at night.

One day I got an email from a corporate executive of a department store. He found my headshot online and wanted to use me for a new advertising campaign. I thought this could be my big break. I met him for lunch across the street from my building we talked about using me to do print ads for women's clothing.

"You're hired," he said, "I'll have a contract for you to sign this weekend." Having worked with men at the club, I was skeptical of this guy. Something was off. There was something about him I couldn't put my finger on. I asked my co-worker to go with me to meet him to sign the papers. There was a cute little bar down the street from my office where we decided to meet that Friday night.

Friday came. I had worked all day; I was so tired. I had not been on any drugs in several days. I was trying to do less and be better. I wanted this contract so bad, so I didn't reschedule the meeting. This was an opportunity for me to make some real money. My co-worker and I met him for a drink. I just sat there. I didn't touch the glass he ordered for me. He had bought it before I got there.

I didn't want to wake up in the hospital again. On and on, he gabbed about nothing. My patience was thin. He made some lame excuses about forgetting the contract, but that it was in his office, really close to where we were.

Across the highway on the other side of the street was the high-rise building, the corporate office of the department store. "You see, the top floor with big windows? That is my office. It is in there," he said. Then he told us his driver could take us over to get it.

I told my friend that I was going to go over to get it and that I would see her tomorrow. I didn't have a cell phone with me, but I figured I would be fine. It looked well-lit. "It would only take a few minutes." We went over to the building. No one, not even security, was there. He pushed the elevator button up and used a keycard for clearance to go to the top floor. The door opened to a room full of desks, chairs, computers, whiteboards, and the usual office stuff.

Around the corner was a door. It was a large wide double door. Inside the door was a long-reaching office with a wall of floor-to-ceiling windows overlooking the parkway and Addison Circle. I could see my office building from there.

I stared out the window as he fumbled around, looking for the papers. He hadn't turned the lights on.

I kept looking out the window, wondering why he would look for something in the dark. Time went by so fast and so slow at the same time; it was almost midnight. I looked down at the parking lot and saw his driver pull away out of the parking lot onto the feeder. The driver had left. He had pulled away and left me there. I started to panic and asked to call my dad. I didn't feel comfortable calling my dad. Our relationship was so messed up. So, I pretended to call. I pushed some buttons on his desk phone, then pretended to talk to someone. "Hi, how are the kids? Ok, well, yes, please come and get me. I am ready." I put down the receiver and looked over as he was shutting the door and, to my horror, was locking it as he whispered to me words I will never forget, "what I want to do here is going to happen." I froze…time stood still. My heart was beating so fast. "I'm so dumb," I thought to myself. "I knew this guy was a creep. This probably isn't even his office. He is probably the f*ing janitor or security guy in a borrowed, ugly brown suit. If he is who he says he is, I was not going to give it up just to be on the cover of some clothing ad! Think fast!"

I looked him right in the eye with full confidence and calmness, which surprised me. And said, "ok," I hopped up onto his desk to sit on top as if I was going to comply with what he wanted from me. He started walking toward me. I saw the real him, a creep with dark eyes and a crooked smile. He took more steps towards the desk and me.

I pointed to the bar across the room. It was on the other side of two sofas and a coffee table, and I said, "you can at least make me a drink first." He turned toward the wet bar; as he passed the sitting area, once he moved far away enough from me and the door, I bolted, lunging my body to the door. I quickly turned the lock flung open the door, and sprinted to the elevator, but it wasn't going to work. I don't have his security card. Just then, I noticed the door to the fire escape, I took it. I flew down the fire escape, down every floor of stairs. There was a lot, but it wasn't even hard. I felt like I literally flew down; I don't remember even touching the ground. I ran out into the street and literally ran all the way home. A man in a pick up truck tried to give me a ride but I was too traumatized. I quietly tiptoed into the room where my kids were sleeping and climbed into bed with them. I was so thankful to be alive. I cried myself to sleep, tears of joy to be home and tears of regret of how dumb I was.

Kidnapped

Memory after doing meth is vague, and the timeline of my drug-induced life is blurred. I heard the house I had with Bill was unoccupied. I moved back in. All the furniture was gone. It was cold and empty. I slept on the floor. The kids moved into my parents' new home down the street. I soon lost my job at DebtPayPro and was surviving on what little I had stored away. The days all mushed together. I was high all the time. Day into the night, there was no distinction between them. I was at the lowest I had ever been. I was devastatingly alone and in the dark.

One day I was invited over to see my grandparents, who were in for a visit. Little did I know I was walking into an intervention. Parents, grandparents, brothers, and even my cousin Donovan was there. They sent my kids to play in the other room as they confronted me. They discussed my options. There was only one option. Leave with Landon, my brother, and my cousin Donovan and move to Phoenix where I was going to do community service or missionary work for a year.

"Heck no! I'm not going. I'm fine. I can't leave town without my babies." I protested that I didn't need help and that I didn't want to be that far away from the kids. My no wasn't accepted. It was enthusiastically denied and shut down.

I was embarrassing my family. I could feel the disappointment and shame as they looked at me. With force, my dad took me by the arm and walked me outside. Landon opened the back door to a red Ultima Nissan where Donovan was already in the passenger seat.

I was resisting the efforts to get me into the car, so he pushed me into the back seat. As soon as I was in, the door slammed, and away we sped into the night. I was pissed but still so high that I rambled on and on about nothing for hours.

Eventually, I could see the border of Mexico from the highway. There was absolutely nothing in sight, just desert as far and wide as your eyes can see.

We broke down in the desert. We had to pull over and call AAA. El Paso was the next town to get towed. We checked into a hotel room and ate dinner at chilis. I had a drink at dinner or maybe more than a few, I can't remember.

What I do remember is not being able to sleep, so I kept ordering pay-per-view. I would later get into so much trouble for charging up my dad's card to pay for silly stuff. The truth is, I was still drugging big time. I had a stash with me that I had decided to save until I could get back to my life in Dallas.

We got to PHX AZ, where all of my brothers' people (masters commission people) were. Masters Commission is a pre-college opportunity for young adults who are looking to find out what they are called to do before jumping from high school right into college. They can spend one year devoted to prayer and community outreach.

All of these young adults stayed in the same apartment complex, sharing apartments. Some of them had 4 or 5 in one. I got my own, I was too old to be there, and I was dangerous.

Landon gave me the key. It was furnished with hand-me-down furniture and the bare necessities. The apartment was in the slums of Phoenix, so you can imagine my shagreen. At least I had a bed and a place I could start over. It was better than I was able to give myself.

I didn't have a phone or money or even clothes. I figured this was just a trick. They weren't going to leave me here. They will bring me back; this was just to scare me into shape. The next morning before the sun was up, Landon was banging on my door, "time for prayer." Ugh, the last thing I want to do is pray, I thought. I didn't have a choice if I wanted to be able to go anywhere outside of this apartment today. This was my only chance to get fresh air.

Masters Commission

The three of us, Landon, Donovan, and myself pulled to a ginormous church parking lot. Phoenix First Assembly was Pastor Tommy Barnett's. This was the master commissions training station. The campus was breathtaking. The fountains, the grassy courtyard, the children's center that was shaped like a big glass dome, the cafeteria, the preschool, a massive sanctuary, an indoor basketball court and full dance room with gym, and the classrooms for master's commission and a coffee shop with lounge.

A new breed of young people actually paying for and putting life on pause to serve the community for a year or more if they wanted. I thought they were all way too nice, especially to me. I did not deserve niceness. I was as old as their teachers; they were all straight out of high school.

My brother was doing his second year, which made him a leader of some magnitude. He introduced me to everyone as his awesome sister, but I knew he didn't really feel that way. I gathered up some money and drove back to Texas as soon as I could. I stole gas to get there. Pumped and dashed at a station in the middle of nowhere. I met two guys who bought me dinner, and I charged two rooms to a credit card I had no intention of paying. I went straight to frechies when I got into town. He let me crash at his house. When my parents heard I was back, they talked to him, and then he convinced me to go back. So back to Phoenix, I went all with in one week.

A few days went by…I was lonely, even though I was surrounded by people. I hated this lonely feeling. It was dark. All of the crap I had done and gone through in Dallas was all seeping into my consciousness. All of the emotions I had drowned with drugs and alcohol were creeping back in. The reality of all the sin, shame, and regret became overwhelming, and I sunk into depression.

I don't use that word lightly; I think that depression is a dark spirit. I take it very seriously. Having a bad day isn't depression. But dwelling in the mindset of a bad day can carry over into your next day and before you know it you have put yourself into a funk and it's all been based on your own feelings.

Thinking you're worthless, isolating yourself from any real connections, and wanting to sleep all day or drink until you pass out is what kind of depression I was in. Too deep to save myself. I had no interest in anything. Everyone is better without me is what I thought. I was in a dark hole.

I gained a lot of weight, and the drugs I had stored away were running out. I was eating so much junk food. If it came out of the vending machine, that is what I wanted. Pure sugar, processed junk food, and a lot of it.

One day Landon let me take the car to the local grocery store. I had a little bit of cash. I bought hair-cutting scissors. My hair had gotten long, and I didn't like that my roots had grown out, so I was going to trim it up myself. I also decided to put eyeliner in my Loui Vuitton purse that my mom bought me for Christmas. I checked out, purchased the scissors, but intentionally didn't pay for the eyeliner and headed for the door. A lady was standing in front of the door and said, "miss can I have you step into my office" yes, I said.

She escorted me into a small closet space office. The walls were blue. Rectangle tables lined the walls with security camera screens on top of them and some files everywhere. She had another employee come in as a witness.

They asked me to sit down. They said they saw me put something in my purse that I didn't pay for, and the cops were on their way. I sat down in one of the chairs and laid my head down on the table. I wanted them to send me away forever. This was it. My cry for help worked. I was hoping the police would call my parents and tell them that I am a thief and then my parents would give up in helping me. The cop arrived quickly and got all my information. I thought I was going to jail or, better yet, sent back to Texas. I had so many tickets that I never paid back in Texas. Maybe they will find out and send me home for the authorities to punish me back there. I had accumulated parking tickets, speeding, running a red light, and one for an expired license, a total amount of about 5k.

I am a goner, for sure. I sat there as the officer looked through my purse. He pulled out the eyeliner I deliberately stole and some cash. He had a puzzled look on his face as he asked me why I would steal when I had enough money to buy it.

Maybe I wanted attention. Maybe It was a cry for help. Maybe I didn't care what happened to me. Maybe I wanted to get caught, maybe I needed a thrill, maybe I thought I could score more drugs somewhere with that six dollars. I had no answer for him. I just shook my head and said, "I don't know." After running my license, he gave it back to me. I was issued a warning, and the store manager said I wasn't allowed to ever come back to any of their stores. I was stunned. Why did they just let me go?! I was a criminal! A thief, a liar, an addict!

I went back to my apartment and decided to finish off the last bit of meth. Lined it up and snorted it down. All gone. I was ready to give myself a haircut. The kid's bathroom was small. You opened the door, and the sink was right there. Just enough room to open the door. I began trimming the ends of my hair. I would make small cuts, and nothing happened, so I started making bigger cuts, but only a little bit of hair fell to the ground. This is so weird. Maybe I bought right-handed scissors, I am a lefty, so it made sense. I switched hands and started cutting again, but only a few hairs fell to the ground. It wasn't working. I grabbed a chunk of hair and made a big blunt cut.

Nothing! I flipped the scissors. Maybe I had them upside down, but still nothing! Right then, Landon walked into my apartment and into the bathroom. I told him what I was doing and how the scissors were a fluke! I gathered my hair from the very top of my head from my forehead to about the middle of my crown, held it up with one hand, and cut it right in half with the scissors, and nothing happened. "see, I yelled; these are the worst scissors ever!" "Deanna," his eyes widened as he lowered my arm and gently took the scissors out of my hands "stop," He picked up a brush, and as he began to brush my hair, it all began to fall out. By the time he was done brushing, my new hairstyle was revealed. I had given myself a mullet! Those were thinning scissors! I had cut myself a mullet! Great, I am fat, sad, alone, and I have a mullet…what a disaster!

I saved up a little bit of cash that my parents would send me, and the first chance I got, I drove back to Texas, 18 hours straight. I pulled into town and used a payphone to call Frenchie. Once I saw him, he saw my disastrous self-overweight, a mullet, and desperate and depressed. He pitied me, but the love wasn't there. He didn't look at me with love anymore. I knew I should not have come back. I didn't belong here or with him anymore. I was chasing an idea of love I was trying to mend a broken piece of myself. The next day I drove back to Phoenix to my fate.

DIVE DEEP

WHEN HAVE YOU BEEN GIVEN ANOTHER CHANCE AT SOMETHING OR WITH SOMEONE? DID YOU TAKE THE DO-OVER FOR GRANTED, OR DID YOU SEIZE THE OPPORTUNITY?

_____

_____

_____

_____

_____

_____

_____

"When you reach the end of your rope, tie a knot and hang on."

Thomas Jefferson

God, Is That You?

The kids were brought to Phoenix. The three of us were to stay in my little apartment. I enrolled them part-time into the church's preschool so that I could follow my brother around and watch him do ministry. Landon put on food drives and block parties. He has the energy of our mom, non-stop engine and hard to keep up with.

I was with him as he went from house to house and neighborhood to neighborhood, knocking on doors and asking people if they needed food, prayer, or help. It was beautiful watching my little brother minister and lead.

I was moved by his passion for people no matter what economic position, race, age, or even when they refused his help and were mean he never stopped. He had left Dallas a teenager and while I had been a wayward sister failing at life, he had immersed himself into ministry and servanthood and in the process had become this amazing man.

Landon has an unbridled love for all those he came in contact with. It was always a question of what we can we do now. What can we do next and how we could make an even bigger impact. What can we do to bless more people?

Day in and day out, we got up early, met at the church for prayer, I checked the kids into preschool, and followed my brother around doing whatever was on his agenda that day.

One morning I was donning my usual tracksuit and hat. A preschool teacher said to me as I was kissing them goodbye, "your kids are sweet, best behaved, and so smart, and.." she continued, "Victoria, your daughter knows all her colors, including pastels. At nap time, she makes all the other kids cots for them." "Thank you," I said. I walked away and wondered how I got such little angels for kids. It had to be a God thing.

I walked over to the church and found a hidden spot where no one would see me up on the balcony, and I sat on the floor against the wall. I would usually find a spot where I wouldn't be seen. A playlist of worship music filled the building as usual. Song after song for an hour, then we can do your duties.

All of the master's commission people spent this time actually praying. There were some who walked up and down the isles praying out loud, some prayed silently, and some sat in the chairs and wrote in their journals. I saw some sitting at the altar with their eyes closed, just meditating, and some sang out loud with the music. All were engaged in prayer.

Not me. I would hide and wait until they were done. Today was no different. I had nothing to say. I have been numb since I told God I was done. As I sat and waited. A song came on called "Worth

It All" the lyrics caught me. I had never heard it before. A woman sang:

I don't understand Your ways.
Oh, but I will give You my song
Give You all of my praise
You hold on to all my pain
With it, You are pulling me closer
And pulling me into Your ways
Now around every corner
And up every mountain
I'm not looking for crowns
Or the water from fountains
I'm desperate in seeking, frantic, believing
That the sight of Your face
Is all that I need
I will say to You
It's gonna be worth it
It's gonna be worth it
It's gonna be worth it all
I believe this

Hearing these words ring out over my head, they somehow seeped into my heart. It was like my soul was saying these words without my permission.

I began to softly cry. Tears began to roll down my cheeks. I realized I hadn't shed a tear in a very long time, and this felt good to finally feel again. Then, I began to sob. I hugged my knees and dropped my head.

For the first time in a long time, I could cry. I wept. I wept over all my mistakes. I recalled and wept over each failure, the abortion, the engagement, the failed marriage the drug addiction, being a terrible mother a stubborn daughter a poor example of a sister. As I cried over these things, I felt a warm blanket wrap around me, so real, but no one was there. I knew it was the arms of the Father. I heard the sweetest whisper say, "everything is going to be alright!"

I questioned with surprise and awe and asked "your still here?" I can't face the Lord; I can't even face myself. I have done bad things.

Even though there was so much regret and shame I could feel love around me, tangibly. It was so unexpected and undeserved. I knew it was God, I remembered what His love, His presence felt like in my soul. This was it. I had pushed Him so far away from me I never thought I would be able to have a relationship with Him again. It was like He knew I needed a long hug.

The love of God engulfed me that day. I gave God all of my pain and failures and He lifted my burdens. I told Him I wasn't sure how to carry on, that I would never be able to forgive myself for my mistakes. I heard the Holy Spirit say that it's not my job to do the forgiving, that it is the Lord's job to forgive. Only His blood washes away sin stains. I received forgiveness and mercy right then.

For the first time in a long time, I had hope. A line of hope was thrown out to me, and I grabbed hold.

DIVE DEEP

WHAT SONG SPEAKS TO YOU? WHAT SONG IN YOUR LIFE HAS BROUGHT YOU THROUGH A ROUGH PATCH?

Could it be that God was using that song to speak to you…?

_____
_____
_____
_____
_____
_____
_____

A lifeline

John Maxwell wrote said "Jesus is our forerunner". A forerunner is a ship that helps guide a vessel to shore through wind and waves when it can't see and helps it get to shore safely. Jesus is my forerunner, he saved me that day. I continue to find refuge under the shadow of His wing and I know I am covered by His righteousness. I can survive this world knowing that He has me in His loving hand.

A new beginning of a brand 'new walk with God. He was my friend when I didn't have one. He cared about me when I didn't care about myself. My advocate, who I could count on to defend me. I felt this overwhelming confidence that God was looking out for me. I never ever want to drift away from His love again. I was so humbled by the event of how he came to my rescue. His arms were wide open, no shame, only love in His embrace.

The next months, I lived them to the fullest. I participated in ministry after years of being estranged to the work of the Lord. I learned how to worship again, I mean really worship, holding nothing back. I would dance, I would sing as loud as I could, I would fall to my knees and cry out, and at times, I would stand and raise my hands as high as possible, raising to my tiptoes as if I could reach heaven. It was a new level a deeper worship than I had had before even in growing up in church. At times I would not say anything but just be in awe of what God was saying to me.

I was so, so thankful! I could hear His voice, I could feel His presence, and there was so much love and acceptance.

You've Got a Friend

I poured myself into my babies and made new friends. One new friend named Emily Ann Geist. She became my best friend. Emily was short and petite, sandy blonde hair with big green eyes. She was a good person. Someone who loved my kids, and they loved her.

She would come over for tea and play with them, and we would talk for hours. Her friendship was definitely God-sent. I had someone to talk to who didn't know about my past. Of course, I would tell her, but it was a fresh start and a clean slate. My first friend in a new place with a new life.

Friendship is laughter, sharing, caring, and confiding in each other. Friendship is a gift from heaven. God puts people in our hemisphere to help us on our path and show us how to live and give. Some friends give good wisdom, and some a shoulder to cry on. Some friends bail us out of a sticky spot. Everyone needs a friend, at least one good one, and I found mine in Emily.

DIVE DEEP
What qualities do you find most important in a friend?
WHO IS YOUR BEST FRIEND? WHAT MAKES THEM STAND OUT FROM THE REST?

___

I didn't grow up in one place, so it was hard to hang onto friends. My parents moved us around, and I had to change schools a lot to give you an idea. The longest I was at one institution was three years, and that was 10-12th grade. It was hard moving so much because everyone already had their best friend. I got used to being the outsider, the new girl. I learned to make friends quickly by being extra friendly and over-enthusiastic.

In 8th grade, I managed to make one friend who was in love with a tall, dark Hispanic boy in our class. Her father owned a lot of land and had immigrants from Mexico working for him. He was a racist.

I had seen and heard things at her house that just didn't sound good or right. She was afraid of what her dad would do if he found who she was in love with him. We began sneaking out of her house late at night so they could meet up. I felt sorry for her. I felt like she was living a romantic tragedy.

I lied to her parents and mine to keep their love alive. We started sneaking out of my house too. One night after everyone was asleep, we took my parents' car to sneak out to meet her boyfriend. The plan was to pick up her boyfriend and his friend Brandon and I would drive them around for a while then go home.

My family had 40 acres with fruit trees, a garden, cattle, and a long dirt driveway. We climbed out of the bathroom window. I put my mom's new Altima Nissan in neutral and pushed it down the mile long driveway. Once we got to the road, I started it up and drove off to rendezvous with the guys.

I had no interest in Brandon. I asked him to just find some good tunes on the radio while I drove the two love birds in the back around while they made out. I was watching the clock and the gas gauge closely. I put some gas into the tank to cover our tracks dropped everyone off and headed home.

We pulled up to the house. The light was on! My parents were awake! My heart was in my throat. Panic flushed over me! What was I going to say? What would they do to me?

I was caught! "Drive, drive, drive!" she screamed. I kept driving past the house. My life is over now, so I will run away to the city and find an abandoned house to sleep in for the night. I had been up all night, and I was exhausted. I needed to lay my head down. Or, I can sleep in the car, but the sun was coming up, and it was too bright. If I could get some sleep, then I would be able to figure out what to do next. We drove into the city.

I couldn't find any place to park and rest. We turned around to go back into our small town. My friend gave me directions to a classmates house where we could use the phone to call her boyfriend for advice. The classmates wanted to ride around too. None of us had ever had this kind of freedom: a car to go wherever. After talking on the phone, we all got in the car to ride around. My friend, her two friends, and I.

As we were pulling out of the driveway, my friend's sister pulled up and yelled at us. "We gotta go now!" she yelled at me. So, I sped away. The sister got into her car and started chasing us. Everyone in my car was panicking.

I was being chased, I picked up speed and took some sharp turns, but nothing was shaking her off me. We ended up on a dirt road, and I was able to pick up the speed even more.

I came up over a hill that curved down to the right. I started fishtail out of control. Once I was over the hill, I spun the car around and parked it on the side of grass between the dirt road and a bobbed wire fence at the bottom of the hill.

I pulled over because I was scared. Dirt and dust filled the air. I almost lost complete control, and I was worried that her sister was going to get hurt if I didn't stop. So, I pulled over, and we waited. The dust began to settle right when I saw her big white car come over the hill. When she spotted us, she slammed on her brakes and lost control of her car. We locked eyes. CRASH!

In the back seat, the classmates in my car pulled me out of the driver's window. I had blood pouring out of the top of my head, so I took my shirt off to stop the bleeding.

Dust and smoke filled the air. My friend's sister was screaming so loud, but I couldn't understand what she was saying. I looked at my mom's car. It was totaled.

My friend wasn't saying anything. They had pulled her from the car too, but she was going in and out of consciousness, and her whole face was smushed and bloody. We held a shirt to her face too. The five of us walked for a long time. We carried her and tried to keep her awake.

We had walked about a mile when a trucker stopped for us and drove us all to a hospital. All I remember is carrying my only friend in 8th grade into the hospital, her sister screaming for someone to help us. We were all covered in blood.

They took her from our arms and rushed her back. I stood in shock. I looked around. Everyone in the waiting room was staring at me. I thought maybe because I was in a bra and jeans. I took a seat; my eyes were so heavy; I was so tired that I slowly fell asleep. I woke up in a hospital room. A nurse was checking my head, and my parents glared at me at the foot of the bed with disappointed eyes. I could have killed everyone. I had stolen and totaled the car.

I wasn't allowed to see my friend again, or any of them for that matter. Her face had gone thru the gear shift. Her nose and cheekbone broke, and they put a metal plate under her eye. I saw her one more time at the courthouse. She glanced at me with her injured face. I felt like the worst friend. I should have protected her. I should have been smarter.

Friendship should be a place where you can stand up for what is morally right and not cave to pressure. A true friend can say no and handle being said no to. I learned a very hard lesson about peer pressure. I knew it was wrong to take my parents' car. It was wrong to sneak out, lie, and go on a high-speed chase jeopardizing life, but I didn't speak up.

Because of my weakness, I hurt my friend. Looking back, I think she would have still been my friend if I had said no to all those things, but I was too scared to lose her, and because of that, I did lose her.

DIVE DEEP

WHAT MAKES A GOOD FRIEND?

_____
_____
_____
_____
_____
_____
_____

The young adults at master's Commission helped the kids and me. Every day in prayer, I got closer to God. Worship became oxygen for my soul. I joined the choir. These people knew how to call down heaven and dive deep into the presence of God. I learned so much about myself and my own spirituality. Day by day, piece by piece, I was getting put back together in the most beautiful way. As my hair grew out, my love for good things grew. I started eating healthy and working out. I felt safe and guarded. I started to love life, myself, and even my ghetto apartment.

Camp meeting time. The entire master's commission group rented a campground. It had lots of outdoor activities and dorm room-style rooms. They let me and the kids come along. All of the people loved Christian and Victoria. They all made us three feels so included.

On one of the last nights there, we had a church service in a little white chapel at the campground. It had wood floors and folding chairs. The service ran long. Lots of praise, worship, and word, then repeat. The kids started getting tired, but there wasn't anywhere to go.

I got a blanket, laid them down in the back corner of the Church, then guarded the area with a few chairs so that no one would step on them with the dim lights, and it was getting so dark outside. Once they were safe and asleep. I knelt to pray beside them.

The service continued, and I stayed in prayer in the corner with my babies as welcome as the kids in the master's commission made me feel I was still different from them. I had kids to think about.

I had a fear of raising kids alone. I started to weep. I had a life-changing experience at that moment. I gave it to God and told him how scared and ill-equipped I felt to raise the kids. The Lord talked to me about my kids. They are why I was still alive. I cried. I am not good enough for them and can't raise them. I don't know how. I am not ready. I have nothing, no husband, no money, horrible credit, and no job. I sobbed and sobbed. What was I going to do? The reality of all of this was so heavy.

Just then, as real as the sun was in the sky, a warm light lit the dark little corner of that chapel where they were sleeping, a light that I could not just feel. Looking back, I can say it was an angel for sure. When I saw the light, it told me not to be afraid and that God would be with me and help me raise them. Wiping tears away from my eyes and snot from my nose, I said, "I don't want to do this without you. I will ruin them without YOU! I give these babies to you, and if you choose to let me raise them, I will, but only if you are with me.

This moment was life-changing. I dedicated my babies that night. God blessed them and gave them right back to me. He told me that he would always protect them. I loved the relationship I had with God. I could hear him; so open, raw and clear.

Whenever I start feeling fearful about my kids, like them driving, dating, leaving for the military and college. Fear would visit me and be like weeds attempting to choke out any flowers of hope I had. I would return to this memory. This Holy moment with God blessing them and, an oath, giving me a forever promise that they are in His hands. Over the years, I have gone straight to counsel with the Lord over all decisions concerning them, and He has been faithful to His word and promise. He has spared my children and protected them, even from me.

"LOVE IS THE CHAIN WHEREBY TO BIND A CHILD TO ITS PARENTS" ABRAHAM LINCOLN

The Move

My brother Landon asked Emily to marry him. They married on the grand lawn of Phoenix First Assembly in front of the water fountain on the grassy knoll. The whole family was together and happy. The kids and I were in the wedding.

Mom and dad told us they were moving to Lake Havasu City to start a church. I had never heard of Lake Havasu and wasn't excited to move. If I was going anywhere, I wanted to be back to Texas, where I could start over. I didn't have a choice in the matter, and even if I had been given a choice, I didn't trust myself yet.

Landon and Emily would move with us and buy their first home. My parents got a duplex. I lived on one side with the kids, while my parents lived on the other with my younger brothers, Stephen and Nathaniel.

Lake Havasu City is like nothing I had ever seen before. Palm trees, mountains, and a lake. No mall, no super stores; it was a small town with plenty of activities outside. This was paradise! There was so much to be thankful for—a new town, a new start and this time I had a best friend in my new sister-in-law.

I worked from home for my mom's company and took care of the kids. Days turned into weeks, and weeks into months. We would have church services in the living room and invite our neighbors. With new freedom I started feeling alone. I was never alone. My family surrounded me, but the demand of master's commission schedule was lifted, and I had a lot of time to think. I wanted someone to share my life with.

Loneliness visited me at night. I started reaching out to old friends in Texas. Myspace was a new thing I discovered to contact the past and meet new people in my town. I could feel myself begin drifting away.

I reconnected with the Frenchie. We both still said I love you to each other, and he came to visit. We both wanted to see if there was anything still there to salvage. I tried to love him again, and I did in a way. I loved the idea of someone loving me. Deep down, I knew it wasn't meant to be, but I didn't want to be alone. My dad came over to my side of the duplex and asked him to leave and never come back. That was the last time I ever saw him.

Loneliness can be your worst enemy. If you can find a group of people to connect with either at the gym or at Church. Healthy people! Not the crowd at the bars and clubs. Then you will be able to keep loneliness away from settling on you.

DIVE DEEP
WHAT ACTIVITIES DO YOU HAVE THAT YOU ENJOY? IS THERE ANYTHING THAT HELPS YOU PASS THE EXTRA TIME IN THE DAY?

_____
_____
_____
_____
_____
_____
_____
_____

The Devils Snare

Life was simple. My world was very small. For the first time as a single mom, I accepted help from the government. I felt like a loser for doing this, but I recognized the relief of the burden that it lifted so that I didn't go to desperate measures to make ends meet. I was determined to fix my future, so I could be self-sufficient and provide for my kids. Not just survive but thrive.

We had a handful of people in this new town join us for services. God was doing something great. We could all feel it.

Have you ever learned something about yourself that you didn't like? I hated that I was weak. Even though I had a friend, a family, a good job, and help with insurance and groceries, I despised the part of me that wanted to be with someone. I was 25 and frustrated, and battling internally with loneliness.

I started drinking at night so that I wouldn't feel alone. I wasn't in pain about my past, but I didn't like being alone. My space friends were so inclusive. There were so many invitations to parties in this new town. Before I knew it, I sabotaged my new beginning. I made all the same kinds of friends that I had in Dallas. You can change locations, but if you haven't claimed victory over your past, the demons you faced will then find you in your new place.

I was hanging out with a girl from myspace who introduced me to a group of mostly married people with kids. They liked to party. The drugs were always out and available to anyone who wanted some. At first, I didn't do any; I would just drink. The more I resisted, the more they would invite me over. Eventually, I quit working for my mom and was hired by one of them as a personal assistant. I thought this would help me in my way of self-sustaining a life without anyone's help. No parents, no government.

I was lonely because I kept quiet about my past. I wanted to lock away all that happened in Texas and never talk about being a stripper, being divorced, having an abortion, becoming an addict, or leaving the faith. I wouldn't share my testimony with anyone. I resolved that God had taken me back into His loving arms, and I never wanted anyone to know about the past. My secrets made me feel separate from those who loved me most, leading to loneliness, drinking and partying, and before I knew it, I was partaking in meth at parties.

On weekdays, I would stay sober. The weekends were full of partying. Meth and cocaine use was different this time. I wasn't living for the high it was just social. I told myself I had it under control. Every time I would do a line, I could hear a voice tell me to stop, and I would tell that voice that it was the last time. Once the weekend ended, I would cry, repent and set out to do better and be clean.

I lost the respect of my family. They knew something was up. I began to make a lot of poor choices. I would pray all the time for help to quit. I would tell myself that I was done then someone would give me a bag at work or at a party.

DIVE DEEP

IS THERE SOMETHING THAT YOU HAVE TRIED TO QUIT BUT NO MATTER HOW HARD YOU TRY IT KEEPS FINDING IT'S WAY BACK INTO YOUR LIFE?

_____
_____
_____
_____
_____
_____

Prayer

Lord, save me, keep me from harm. I need you to restore my sight so I may see what You see. Give me Wisdom

Amen

Intervention #2

The whole family took a ski trip together to Lake Tahoe for Christmas. Little did I know it was also another intervention. I sat in a chair in the middle of the room as they took turns yelling at me and throwing insults. It didn't work, I knew I deserved it, but I hated them for talking to me like that in front of my kids. I was trying to be good. They didn't know I wanted to quit.

It wasn't the same black hole as in Dallas. I could feel hope, love, and God, but I couldn't break the habit. Snorting meth gave me energy and distracted me from my loneliness. Looking back, that intervention helped a little bit because I cut back on the drugs after that trip.

One day at work, my dad walks in, dressed in a long black dress coat. He strolls right past me into my boss's office. I saw them exchange words then he left without talking to me. I was asked to resign after that, my job there was done. I was given a nice car as a parting gift, and that was it.

My drug habit dwindled to just every once in a while. I started my own business called Spit Spot because I love Mary Poppins.

A whirlwind of changes, I moved in with a boyfriend who was part of the group of friends I made in town, he had some demons. I consider this relationship the shortest and grossest one ever. Let's just say he was battling his identity, and drugs exposed the ugly. While we were living with him. I started wanting to go back to Church and begged him to go over and over.

One Sunday morning, after fighting all night about where he had been. He would just disappear, and it brought back so much hurt from my past relationships. I wasn't going to put up with this again. I had seen his phone records and confronted him. Once the fighting was over, he fell asleep, promising to go to Church with me. I was up early, ready to go, but he never got up. I'll ask one more time, I said to myself. I walked into the room and said, "It's time to go. Are you coming?" He said clearly and firmly, "I will never go to your parents' Church." I said, "Ok, then I am done." It was what I needed to hear to move on. I had to choose him or my family, him or my faith, him or my Church. It was easy. I didn't choose him. I packed up all the kid's things and most of mine and left. As I pulled away, it was the best feeling I had had in a long time. One good decision I made on my own.

One Good Choice Can Save Your Life

I lived in a house that a nice old man at Church had available, then moved into a rental that I could afford with my cleaning business. A few different people were pursuing me. One was a doctor, one was a business owner. I didn't want anyone. I wanted to keep making good choices and leaning more into God. I had almost broken free of drugs completely.

I went to a local bar. I had a yellow dress on that I had borrowed. I was with a group of people. As I walked through the crowd to find a table, I saw a guy standing above everyone on a box. He was a bouncer. He had broad shoulders, dark hair and was standing with his arms folded across his chest, watching me walk by down below.

When we made eye contact, my heart jumped out of my chest. I was holding hands with a guy friend who was guiding me through the mass of people. I shook my hand free and asked this striking bouncer to lean down. I hadn't thought this through at all. He did. What was I going to do now? I got onto my tiptoes, pulled my face to his ear and bit his neck! What a dumb idea, I thought! He is going to think I'm crazy.

Even more panicked now, I took off. I ran and hid in the crowd. I felt so dumb. Why in the world did I bite him? He is probably so weirded out. I am such an idiot.

I would do drugs for energy. I learned to sleep and drink while being able to do drugs. I could hear God's voice still, and I would cry and repent and swear I wouldn't do drugs again, and then I would get a bunch of it for free either from a client or a supposed friend who wanted a party partner.

There he was again another night at the local bar, he was working. He was dressed in a costume, a silly cop outfit for Halloween. It made me second-guess my feelings about him the costume wasn't my favorite especially a cop one. I played it cool and sat still. I waited to see if he would notice me. Even though he was working, he made a point to come to talk to me. His name was Jared. He asked for my number & I apologized for biting him.

Some time went by my cleaning business was doing good. I had distanced myself from a lot of the poor-quality friends, save a few. The Church was growing, and I was participating now.

I was carrying so much shame for not being able to stay clean. I felt the Holy Spirit with me and convicting me every time. I wanted to stop so badly.

One good decision after another leads to a rhythm of grace.

One day my phone rang. I had been sober for a few weeks. It was Jared. He said he had tried calling some of his closer friends, but no one was answering. He needed someone to talk to.

Someone close to him had committed suicide, and he was really upset about it. I felt so bad for him. I listened and cried as he told me how it happened and the last time he spoke to his friend.

He asked me why this would happen, how to recover and how to make sense of it. This was the first conversation I had ever had with Jared, and it was very deep. I didn't want him to be alone, and I could tell he wasn't in a good mental space to be alone. But I didn't know him and wanted to make better choices on who I brought around the kids. The kids were at my parents' house, so I invited him over.

There was something different about Jared. He was bold and a little intimidating, but when he spoke, he was kind, big-hearted, and gentle. He is so smart and handsome. He feels things very deeply. He is honest and real. I told him that night that my relationship with God was weak, and I didn't have the answers, but I knew if he went to church, I could introduce him to someone who could help. He asked me what church I went to. I told him it was my family's. We had been meeting on Sundays at the Ramada Inn conference room. He was surprised to hear that because it was the same church his coworker Ezekiel had invited him to. He agreed to go.

Jared is good. The goodness in him was better than I deserved. I had been a single mom for seven years. He swept me off my feet. My heart raced when I looked at him. One of the sweetest things was when he would hug me, and his arms would shake. He said I made him nervous. As I got to know him, I realized he had more passion inside of him than anyone I had ever known.

I was on the worship team singing when he walked into church. He couldn't take his eyes off me. Emily asked if I knew him and why he stared so hard at me. I told her I met him at the bar. We started seeing one another. I moved in with my parents. I enrolled in school at MCC and decided to become a Dental Assistant.

I was still talking to a guy in bullhead and trying to keep contact with Frenchie at the same time I was talking to Jared. I was having a hard time moving on from Frenchie. It was like I was trying to fix something in the past or maybe fix something inside of me. It had been years since I left Texas, but I was still wondering about all the what-ifs.

At Christmas, I had Jared come to my parents' house and take pictures of the kids and me. I got us all dressed up and sat under the tree.

The pictures turned out so good that I emailed them to Frenchie. What would he say about them, I wondered. I wanted him to have regrets like I did. I wanted him to miss me and be haunted by what could have been.

Every year since the abortion, I have dreams of my baby and Frenchie. Weird pregnancy dreams, scary ones, some of an alternate future. They would begin in March and stop right around the due date.

I resolved that I would carry the guilt, shame, and torture that killing a baby had. I deserve to be tormented. I would keep the abortion, the stripping, and all the other things I had done a secret from everyone other than my family and Jared. But no one else could know. My life story is closed.

I brought all my baggage to Jared and let him sort through it. It wasn't fair or right. Jared had grace for the past but was not ok with me keeping a relationship with Frenchie. This brought tension instead of strength to our new relationship. I had to apologize, make it right, and promise to be loyal to him and stop looking back at the past. He deserved and had earned that respect.

It wasn't until I decided to be transparent with any and all about my testimony, the things I had done, and the person I had been that our love grew into something deeper than I could imagine. When I got to this maturity in my journey with myself it opened up doors I never knew would open for me. Opportunities in ministry. A deeper love and appreciation in my marriage and more blessings than I could contain.

DIVE DEEP

THERE WAS A WOMAN IN THE BIBLE WHO WAS INSTRUCTED TO LEAVE AND NOT LOOK BACK. GOD WAS SAVING HER, BUT IT CAME WITH INSTRUCTIONS NOT TOO LONG OR EVEN LOOK BACK. HER DISOBEDIENCE COST HER LIFE.

WHAT IS IN YOUR REARVIEW MIRROR THAT YOU NEED TO STOP LOOKING AT?

_____
_____
_____
_____
_____
_____
_____

Be sure your sins will find you out:

The cops pulled me over in Lake Havasu. I handed them my Texas ID even though I had an AZ license. I had too many unpaid tickets, so I rolled the dice, thinking they wouldn't know.

They arrested me for driving under a suspended license. All my tickets from Texas caught up to me. They took me away. I spent three days in Kingman prison. I deserved more jail time than that. The day I was arrested, I had a known drug dealer/friend of my cousin in my car.

One time a cop and a drug dog searched the house I was staying in. I had a pile of meth that I rubbed into the carpet in panic. I should have gone away for that, or when they took me in for questioning about the people I was rolling with, I got patted down, and I had a huge bag of meth in my bra. When the female officer unclasped my bra, I thought my life was over. My life flashed before my eyes. I thought about how much time in jail I would get and how crappy my life would be. I desperately and swiftly pleaded to God right then, "God, if you spare me, I will live my life for you forever." The bag stuck to my skin. The officer was done with the search, and I got dressed.

The following day, I walked out of that jail with the drugs still on me. I deserved a sentence much longer than three days.

Jared drove me to Kingman. He watched the kids for the three days. I cried and slept most of the time inside. There was one sock and sandal softball game with the inmates. I couldn't even try to play; I just sat in the corner. The other inmates tried to make me feel better. Some of them had been there for ninety days. I swore this was my wake-up call.

Jared picked me up when it was over. He still believed in me. He still looked at me as if I was pure and beautiful. He looked at me the way I used to see myself, before everything.

When he looked at me, it was as if he saw me the way I believe God sees me. God sees us just as we are but also sees the uniqueness. He knows the real you, the you He created. He placed in us HIS goodness. God places intrinsic value on every one of His children.

I don't deserve Jared. I don't deserve God and His goodness. I broke every moral code and every commandment, but somehow, He still saw me worthy, and Jared was sent to help me on my way.

My brother Landon and my father baptized Jared in the lake. On the way out of the water Landon looked at me and told me Jared was the best one I had ever picked. "I didn't pick him yet," I retorted, although deep down, I was relieved that I finally found someone my family approved of. I was worried that I would ruin it.

DIVE DEEP

When you are vulnerable the people closest to you sometimes have the best advice. Who can you trust to give you sound advice?

_____
_____
_____
_____
_____
_____
_____

Is it Over?

I got a one-bedroom apartment. It was a new beginning again for us. Jared left to get some things from the store and was coming back to help me move in. I started to feel tired. I remembered I had a little meth left. I poured it onto the counter. I told myself I didn't want drugs in this new life or this new apartment. I promised myself this was the last time. I would move all the stuff in stop doing drugs and start fresh.

Jared walked in, went straight to the bathroom, and saw the little bag in the toilet that hadn't flushed and my driver's license on the counter that I had used to line it up. He was shocked. His face showed not only his disgust but disappointment.

I rattled off that I was done with it, that I wanted to quit, and was just finishing off what was left. That I was glad he caught me. He was speechless and left me standing there. It was over.

As I watched out the patio door, he got in his car and pulled away. I sunk into the corner of the room, hugged my knees, dropped my head, and began crying. I surprised myself, before this I was never be able to cry on drugs; this was new, and I wept. I didn't feel sorry for myself at all. I felt bad for Jared, he trusted me and I let him down. I was a terrible person.

I prayed in the corner of the room that God would protect Jared from me. He was a new believer and had a great start on his Christian walk, and now the hypocrite of a preacher's daughter has ruined it.

Please, God, don't let him leave You. It's ok if he leaves me, but please keep him close to You. I will never do drugs again, even if Jared hates me forever. I am done with drugs forever. Just don't let me ruin his walk with You, Lord.

As I continued to cry, not sure how long I was there when the door opened. Jared walked inside the empty apartment. He asked me questions… how long…who I got it from…how many lies... I told him everything.

He didn't tell me we were ok or that we could still be together. He just listened and then left again.

Forever Changed

Sunday was Easter Sunday. I bought a white dress to signify my new life of being drug-free. Once and for all, I wasn't ever going back. I sang my heart out that Sunday, and I noticed Jared. He was there. I never again wanted or longed for drugs or alcohol ever again. I was finally free.

Secret sins fester. When light shines, darkness has to flee. Whatever is done in the dark will be brought to light, and when that happened to me, it changed me forever.

God was doing something new in and through both of us. Jared would come over and help me study and play with the kids. We would talk for hours.

Is this what real love is? Is it knowing and seeing the ugliest parts of someone and loving them still? Is real love this easy and this hard? No one had loved me like this before. He thinks I'm prettier without makeup. His mouth falls open when I sing, he looks at me like I am a pure..that the drugs and the past aren't what he sees when he looks at me. I was in love deeper than I ever knew possible. He knew everything about me and still wanted to be with me.

Jared asked for my hand in marriage, and we started pre-marital counseling. In counseling, he brought up some people I had not cut off communications with. He pleaded his case to the counselor to get an outside opinion. My stance was that I was a new person whom I felt I could witness to. Our counselor took Jared's side, this person did not want my help and didn't want me to stop partying.

Dive Deep

The saying, "misery loves company" is true. Some people are only your friend if you stay in their disfunction. Do you have the courage to grow and become better even if it means saying goodbye to some people in your life?

_____
_____
_____
_____
_____
_____
_____

I wrote a letter to this particular person and parted ways for good. Having Jared was a godsend. I recognized the wisdom in the man God had entrusted me to. I would marry him. His family embraced me like I was their own. I love his whole family! He dedicated his life to the kids and, of course, to me. We are far from perfect. But we are right where God wants us to be.

DIVE DEEP

HOW DID YOUR LOVE STORY BEGIN? IF IT HASN'T YET, WHAT DO YOU ENVISION FOR YOUR FUTURE RELATIONSHIP?

_____
_____
_____
_____
_____

The Taste of VICTORY

"NO VICTORY WITHOUT SUFFERING"
J.R.R. TOLKIEN

What the enemy meant for evil. God used it for good. I have personal victories in addiction, regrets, shame, insecurity & unworthiness. Victory tastes great! Victory shared is even better! I know it is not only God's grace but also my family who deserve the praise for my freedom.

I am surrounded by warriors. My mother and father, my brother Landon my best friends Emily and Jared fought for me when I couldn't fight for myself. They fought to save my life and the kids' future. Since then, we have multiplied. My other two brothers married and had kids. My daughter married and gave us a grandbaby boy. Our tribe is strong. We stand united together, shoulder to shoulder, fighting the good fight.

I had been trapped in a dark cave, and it took a village to save me. It took my family to get me out into the light.

This is my story a story of redemption. If you struggle with additions and bad habits that are hard to break there is HOPE. Many years later my love for God and the things of God has soared to levels I never dreamed imaginable. I exist on this planet as an example of the wonder and magnificence of God.

By His great grace, I am alive. My heart is open to those around me and what I've done is not a secret. I've been backslidden, a prodigal, a liar, a cheat, a thief, and a murderer. I've dishonored my parents, abandoned my children, divorced, and been an addict. BUT GOD! BUT GOD! BUT GOD!

Now, I am in full-time ministry as the Pastoral oversight for worship, women, youth, and speaking. I pray every day that God helps me to love and lead His people the way He wants.

If the Lord can make a way for me, He can do it for you. There is nothing that can separate you from His love, no, not anything!

I pray that my story gives you hope and brings you closer to His heart. Do not give up on your loved ones who may be dabbling in darkness. God can and will work all things for your good, bring you into a life full of endless possibilities, and give you the desires of your heart. Finally most of all I pray... Father, I surrender. Fill me with your Holy Spirit. I don't want to go another moment without you in my life. Thank you for forgiving me, saving me, and redeeming me.

AMEN

May the God of hope fill you with all joy as you trust him so that you may overflow with HOPE by the power of the Holy Spirit.
Romans 15:13

LIFE LESSONS : Discussion time

A community of healthy people around you can protect you from poor choices
James 5:16 Therefore confess your sins to each other and pray for each other so that you may be healed. The prayer of a righteous person is powerful and effective.

God gives multiple chances
1John 1:9 "If we confess our sins, he is faithful and just to forgive us our sins and to cleanse us from all unrighteousness."

God waits till you're ready to receive

1Corinthians 13:4 "Love is patient and kind; it is not jealous or conceited or proud; it is not arrogant."

Wounds must be treated and healed ALL the WAY
Psalms 6:2 "Have mercy on me, Lord, for I am faint. Heal me, Lord, for my bones are in agony."

Forgive others and forgive yourself.
Ephesians 4:32 "Be kind and compassionate to one another, forgiving each other, just as in Christ God forgave you."

Move forward. Don't bring hurt into a new relationship.
Your "x" is an "x" for a reason, but it doesn't have to be messy. You have a choice.
Matthew 10:16 "Behold, I send you out as sheep in the midst of wolves; so be shrewd as serpents and innocent as doves."

God isn't mean. He isn't hateful.
1 John 4:7-8- Dear friends, let us continue to love one another, for love comes from God. Anyone who loves is a child of God and knows God. But anyone who does not love does not know God, for God is love.

Your loved ones can be pushed to do things they would never want to do but are forced to because of the trauma you have put them through

John 15:13 - There is no greater love than to lay down one's life for one's friends.

A real man, the right man, will look at you like you are the Eve that God created just for him, untouched and sacred.

Matthew 19:6 "So they are no longer two, but one flesh. Therefore what God has joined together, let no one separate."

Addiction is real, BUT so is GOD, and addiction can be overcome with faith and love, and a Promise

Corinthians10:13 "No temptation has overtaken you that is not common to man. God is faithful, and he will not let you be tempted beyond your ability, but with the temptation he will also provide the way of escape, that you may be able to endure it."

Thessalonians5:6-8 "So then, let us not be like others, who are asleep, but let us be awake and sober. For those who sleep, sleep at night, and those who get drunk, get drunk at night. But since we belong to the day, let us be sober, putting on faith and love as a breastplate, and the hope of salvation as a helmet."

The things you have done or have been done to your kids can be healed and repaired by honesty and love.

Psalms 127:3 "Children are a gift from the Lord; they are a reward from him."

Some people are not good for you. Let them go. You have to save yourself before you can save anyone else

1 Corinthians 15:33, NLT: Don't be fooled by those who say such things, for 'bad company corrupts good character.

Let the Holy Spirit be your ultimate counsel.

Isaiah 11:2 The Spirit of the LORD will rest on him— the Spirit of wisdom and of understanding, the Spirit of counsel and of might, the Spirit of the knowledge and fear of the LORD—

Made in the USA
Las Vegas, NV
02 May 2023

71468575R00085